CONVERSATIONS ON THE LOST CONNECTION WITH NATURE

MONIQUE PARKER

Understanding the Importance of Nature
and the Need for (Re)Connection

BALBOA.PRESS
A DIVISION OF HAY HOUSE

Copyright © 2023 Monique Parker.

All rights reserved. No part of this book may be used or reproduced by any means, graphic, electronic, or mechanical, including photocopying, recording, taping or by any information storage retrieval system without the written permission of the author except in the case of brief quotations embodied in critical articles and reviews.

Balboa Press books may be ordered through booksellers or by contacting:

Balboa Press
A Division of Hay House
1663 Liberty Drive
Bloomington, IN 47403
www.balboapress.co.uk
UK TFN: 0800 0148647 (Toll Free inside the UK)
UK Local: (02) 0369 56325 (+44 20 3695 6325 from outside the UK)

Because of the dynamic nature of the Internet, any web addresses or links contained in this book may have changed since publication and may no longer be valid. The views expressed in this work are solely those of the author and do not necessarily reflect the views of the publisher, and the publisher hereby disclaims any responsibility for them.

The author of this book does not dispense medical advice or prescribe the use of any technique as a form of treatment for physical, emotional, or medical problems without the advice of a physician, either directly or indirectly. The intent of the author is only to offer information of a general nature to help you in your quest for emotional and spiritual well-being. In the event you use any of the information in this book for yourself, which is your constitutional right, the author and the publisher assume no responsibility for your actions.

Any people depicted in stock imagery provided by Getty Images are models, and such images are being used for illustrative purposes only.
Certain stock imagery © Getty Images.

Print information available on the last page.

ISBN: 978-1-9822-8743-6 (sc)
ISBN: 978-1-9822-8742-9 (e)

Library of Congress Control Number: 2023914091

Balboa Press rev. date: 08/03/2023

In memory of *Han & Riet*
My parents who always encouraged me to follow my dreams

CONTENTS

It All Started with the Cosmos.. xi

Introduction.. xv

Part 1   Nature & Health.. 1

Part 2   Nature & Nutrition... 25

Part 3   Conversations on the Lost Connection with Nature............. 49

- Meet Abby – Green Hub Volunteer and A-level student......... 57
- Meet Amir – Physics professor-turned-farmer in Iran 62
- Meet Andrew – Beekeeper and Retired RHS Principal Entomologist 66
- Meet Charlie – Yoga teacher and Designer 70
- Meet Daniel – Nutritionist, Functional Medicine Practitioner & Author... 75
- Meet Daria & Heine – Founders of the Bliss & Stars Retreat in South Africa... 81
- Meet Ed – Botanist, Managing Director of Aquasol (botanicals) and Director of Bionutri Ltd............................... 87
- Meet Élise – Biology Graduate and Traveller from Canada..... 94
- Meet Emily – Forager and Documentary Producer................. 99
- Meet Fred – Agro-ecological Farmer..................................... 106

- Meet Guy – Organic Farmer, Founder of Riverford - an organic farm and organic vegetable box delivery company, and 'self-confessed veg nerd' 114
- Meet Jenny – Medical doctor, Author, Lecturer and Broadcaster 120
- Meet Jim – Nature lover, medical director and retired family physician from the USA... 130
- Meet Joe – Entrepreneur and former pro swimmer 136
- Meet Lou – Naturopath, Adventurer and Skydiver 141
- Meet Mariel & Gerbrand – Owners and Guardians of the 'Mengelmoestuin' in the Netherlands 147
- Meet Marion – Beekeeper & Retired Biologist 151
- Meet Mel – Owner of a Zero Waste & Refill Shop and Mother of Three 154
- Meet Olivier – Naturopath, Nutritional Therapist and Naturopathic Chef..158
- Meet Orli – Nurse, Trauma-informed Massage Therapist, Writer, Artist, Dancer, and Mother to four free-spirited souls..163
- Meet Phoebe – Nutritional Therapist, Clinical Director, Product & Recipe Developer 171
- Meet Sophie – Marketeer turned Horticulturist and Mother-to-be*.. 177
- Meet Susan – Acupuncturist, Chinese Herbalist & keen ice-skater...181
- Meet Thinley – Bhutanese Traditional Medicine Practitioner... 186
- Meet Tone – Chiropractor, Founder of Luck's Yard Clinic and Co-founder of The Green Hub Project for Teens 190
- Meet Victoria – Director of Silverwoods Forest School and Mother of One..195
- Meet Zarah* – Trauma Survivor and Nature-lover 200

Part 4	The Disconnection from Nature	207
Part 5	How to (Re)Connect with Nature	215

Epilogue	225
Acknowledgements	227
References	229
About the Author	245

IT ALL STARTED WITH THE COSMOS....

'Some memories are unforgettable, remaining ever vivid and heart-warming!'

Joseph B. Wirthlin
American Businessman

By Cosmos, I do not mean the Universe here, although, when you think about it, it all started with that too, of course. No, what I'm talking about are those lovely flowers, ranging in colour from white through to pink, red and orange, with the yellow centres, that happen to be part of the sunflower family.

Trying to grow as much from seed as possible, I almost thought we wouldn't succeed again this year, after having all Cosmos seedlings decimated by slugs last year. 'Keep trying' is our motto, and it worked. By planting the seedlings in a different part of our garden, we were rewarded with an abundance of flowers, still going strong in October. And it was these lovely flowers that gave me the idea for this book, and here is the reason why.

I grew up in The Hague, the third-largest city in the Netherlands, in an area full of concrete flats. Living in a small top-floor flat, with my parents and brother, we had just a narrow balcony at the back, overlooking the ground-floor flats' gardens. Sitting on the balcony, you had to sit in a row, but at least it was outdoors.

Mum created a mini garden with several window boxes filled with geraniums and other colourful plants. It was lovely, but we still looked with some envy at the gardens below.

The flats were situated along a canal with flats either side, and houseboats on the full length of the canal. It was a rather built-up area and the only greenery, apart from the ground-floor flats' gardens, consisted of some trees lining the pavement.

I sometimes wonder if my parents were feeling claustrophobic in that city flat, as every chance they had to take us out into Nature was grabbed with both hands.

So, what does the Cosmos have to do with all this?

When I was in primary school, I joined the school allotment club.

I was craving Nature and the window boxes on our balcony were just not enough for me.

This allotment club was located at the Children's Farm in the Zuiderpark, a huge park with 105 hectares of green space, that happened to be walking distance from my school.

After school, a teacher would take a small group of us to the allotment, and we learned about growing vegetables and flowers. I will never forget how proud I was when I harvested my first carrots! The flowers I grew, you can probably guess, were Cosmos. Growing in between my potatoes and carrots and growing as tall as I was myself at the time. It was my little green paradise, my happy place.

Seeing the Cosmos doing so well in our garden this year, suddenly reminded me of my childhood and how happy that tiny school allotment made me. It was a little bit of Nature just for me.

I started reminiscing about the sixty-two trips around the sun I have made so far, and if there had been more memorable connections with Nature during that time. It didn't take long for me to make the connection between my happiest times in life and the importance Nature played in all of them.

Nature is my healer, my go-to when I'm feeling down and my charging station when I'm tired. Nature amazes me every single day and it makes me feel alive. I could go on and on.

Through my work as a naturopathic nutritional therapist, I have encountered quite a number of people who are rather disconnected from Nature, but I'll explain that further in the next chapter.

It is not just my clients who have motivated me to write this book. It's also what is going on in our world right now. As a nutritional therapist I obviously have a strong interest in food.

There are many concerns involving our complex food system that must be addressed, like its sustainability, the way we deal with food waste, the control and economics of food production, how food production affects our natural environment, and the influence of food on people's health. However, it is not just our food system that concerns me. Climate change and sustainability are much on my mind too. After all, we are talking about the future of our planet.

In my view, understanding the importance of Nature in our world and our personal lives is a first step to connecting with Nature, as it positively affects pro-environmental and responsible behaviour. This cannot start early enough.

On a more positive note, there are many people who are strongly connected with Nature, some of them from as early as childhood. I have been very lucky to meet a group of inspirational individuals, who all, through profession or personality, have a strong bond with Nature that brings them joy and fulfilment. They all agreed to share their thoughts about 'The Lost Connection with Nature', and have given permission to get it published, for which I am eternally grateful. I hope you will enjoy their stories as much as I did.

In her book *Grounded*, Ruth Allen wrote, "What Nature means to you will be uniquely based on your experience being alive in the world".

Everyone's story will be different.

INTRODUCTION

*'We are all meant to be naturalists,
each in his own degree, and it is inexcusable to
live in a world, so full of marvels of plant and animal life
and to care for none of these things'.*

*Charlotte Mason
British Educator and Reformer*

Why is it so important to be connected with Nature? And why is it so worrying that more and more people seem to be out of tune with Nature?

A lot has been written about the importance of Nature for us human beings, but of course we will all have our own ideas about this. Some people see Nature just as a provider of life's necessities: air, water, the food we eat, etc., or the bringer of disasters such as earthquakes, tsunamis, drought and so on. Others have a strong spiritual connection with Nature, and they live their lives in tune with its rhythms and cycles. Artists find inspiration in Nature; others find solace in Nature when the world does not make sense.

But no matter how we look at it, we are all connected with Nature, from the air that we breathe to the technology that helps us to be effective. Believe it or not, we are connected to Nature, even through our mobile phones, as they contain up to 16 out of the 17 rare earth metals such as neodymium or dysprosium, for which there are currently no suitable alternatives.

One view on Nature is from Ralph Waldo Emerson, a nineteenth century American philosopher, who wrote in his essay, 'Nature,' that both man and Nature are expressions of the divine, and that Nature was made to serve man's physical, intellectual, and spiritual needs. Man and Nature share a special bond.

More contemporary is a study conducted by the University of Derby in 2020 on pro-Nature conservation behaviours, showing the crucial importance of a close connection with Nature, and engagement with Nature through simple activities that improve the bond with Nature, and help to care for and save our planet.

To me one of the most interesting views on Nature comes from the American author Richard Louv. In his book, *The Nature Principle: Human Restoration and the End of Nature-Deficit Disorder*, he concludes that the benefits of Nature to our health and awareness will be immaterial if we keep on ruining our natural environment. The destruction of Nature is guaranteed if we do not reconnect to Nature.

We all have a personal definition of Nature, based on our own experiences. Look at art, read books, listen to music, and you will find that people are inspired by Nature to express their emotions and thoughts. To me Nature is the Universe, Life, and the greatest inspiration. We are all part of Nature whether we like it or not. As the American writer Joseph Campbell said, "…the goal of life is to make your heartbeat match the beat of the universe to match your Nature with Nature."

What I would like to address in this book is the special relationship we all have, consciously or unconsciously, with Nature, its benefits for our health and well-being, and the necessity to restore the lost connection to save our planet and our future. After all, Nature underpins our very existence; we are an intrinsic part of Nature.

Part of this book contains the conversations I had on this topic with twenty-seven inspirational people, who are all strongly connected with Nature, through profession or personality.

However, before diving into all these wonderful, inspiring stories, I would like to show you the connection between Nature and health, and – impossible not to mention as a nutritional therapist – the link between Nature and nutrition.

PART ONE

NATURE & HEALTH

'The health of soil, plant, animal and man is one and indivisible'

Lady Eve Balfour
Founder of the Soil Association

There is a tremendous amount of research available on all aspects of the connection between Nature and health. So much has been written about this valuable connection, going back as far as the ancient Greeks, possibly even much further. One of the many famous quotes by Hippocrates, the Greek physician (475 – 360 BCE) is, "…ill health is a disharmony between man and his environment". Our Greek friend already saw at the time, that human health and wellbeing are intimately linked to the state of the environment. Many of his writings survived over time, showing that his medical approach was based on the healing power of Nature, and I'm sure that Hippocrates also knew that while humans couldn't survive without Nature, Nature could survive without human beings.

There is someone else I would like to mention here too, a remarkable German woman who lived in the 12th century, and who had a very clear vision on the connection between Nature and health. Her name was Hildegard von Bingen, and besides being a Benedictine abbess, she was also a visionary, writer, composer, philosopher, and a medical practitioner.

Working in the monastery's herbal garden, her practical experience with patients, and all the knowledge she had gained from the books in the monastery's library, made her combine all she had learned, both in theory and practice, in two publications / major works: *Physica,* a series of nine books in which she writes about the medicinal and scientific qualities of about 500 plants, stones, metals, elements and animals used in about 2000 remedies, and *Causae et Curae*, in which she describes connections between the human body and Nature, and the origin of diseases and their cure.

Hildegard was definitely a formidable lady, whose books have inspired many practitioners throughout time. However, the most important reason for mentioning Hildegard in this context, is because of her concept of 'Viriditas', meaning greenness, or the divine force of Nature, which is found in all her work. Hildegard lived her entire life in a green valley near the River Rhine in Germany, and this must have had a significant impact on her, as she saw the greenness of Nature as a metaphor for physical and spiritual health. Hildegard had the view that the human body was like a plant. Plants have the extraordinary ability to regenerate, the 'greening power' or 'Viriditas'. The human body has its own 'Viriditas'.

Before moving on to other aspects of Nature and health, I would like to share with you a beautiful quote from Hildegard:

*"Glance at the Sun. See the Moon and the stars.
Gaze at the beauty of Earth's greenings.
Now, think.
What delight God gives to humankind
with all these things.
All Nature is at the disposal of humankind.
We are to work with it.
For without we cannot survive."*

NATURAL RHYTHMS

To have a good understanding of the effects of Nature on health, it is important to look at the natural rhythms. Although our world is naturally chaotic and volatile, the cycles or rhythms of Nature are giving us balance. Think about the day-night cycle, the sleep-wake cycle or the lunar cycle; we know that after the dark of night there will be the light of day, and we know that the moon is always there, watching us, even when it is a New Moon and we can't see the moon, we know it is there, but it is just not facing its side that is lit up by the Sun.

All these cycles are part of the circadian and seasonal rhythms that affect all living beings, including animals, plants, and microbes. As soon as there is an imbalance in the rhythms, the problems begin.

The Body Clock

Most people are awake during the day and asleep at night, unless they're working night shifts of course, are suffering from jetlag, having sleep issues or if they are very young babies or teenagers.

Babies do not have a circadian rhythm like adults until they are about 3-4 months old, hence their often-erratic sleeping patterns. Some babies are bad sleepers until they're much older, but this has more to do with their developmental changes, colds, viruses, teething, etc. Broken nights are a parent's worst nightmare, as they disrupt their circadian rhythm and leave them exhausted during the day, an experience I remember well, having a daughter who didn't sleep through the night until she was three years old!

Teenagers have a circadian rhythm that is also different from that of adults, because of the way teenage hormones respond to light and darkness exposure. This influences their body clocks, making them want to stay up later at night and sleep longer in the morning. It is not always laziness, trust me. No matter what your circadian rhythm is like, being a lark or an owl, an adult or a teenager, school and offices start at times that are often demanding. For most teenagers starting school at 8.30am is hard, as they are often sleep-deprived because of their shifted sleeping pattern. Research has shown that teenagers perform best in the afternoon, whereas adults don't do as well in the afternoon. Maybe it is time for schools to adjust their timetables?

The Light-Dark Cycle

Our body responds to light and dark, just like most other living beings. Our biological or body clocks regulate the cycle of circadian rhythms, the physiological, mental, and behavioural changes that happen to us throughout a 24-hour day. The circadian rhythm is our body's daily timekeeper.

Almost every tissue and organ in the body has these biological clocks that are made up of certain molecules, proteins, that work with cells in the body.

Scientists have discovered that fruit flies have genes that are similar to the genes that control the human body clock, so it is no surprise that the little fruit fly and its body clock have been extensively researched.

In 2017 three scientists won the Nobel Prize in Physiology or Medicine for their research in molecular mechanisms controlling the circadian rhythm. The research was done on, you can probably guess, fruit flies. The scientists discovered the 'period gene', which encodes a protein at night that tells our body that it is time to go to sleep. The protein builds up in cells during the night, and then breaks down during the day, so you won't go to sleep during that time. Oscillating genes, like the 'period gene', that control our circadian rhythm, are expressed in a cycle of about 24 hours. These genes are moving back and forth in a regular rhythm.

Whether you're an early bird or a night owl depends largely on what genes you have that regulate your circadian rhythm. Genetic research has shown that there are 351 genes that regulate this rhythm, but you don't necessarily have all of them. A study using genome-wide data from 697,828 participants showed that the 5% of people with the most circadian rhythm genes were going to bed 25 minutes earlier than the 5% who have the fewest. Consumption of alcohol, caffeine and nicotine also seems to have an effect. Apparently, night owls consume more of these substances than early birds.

All our body clocks are regulated by a master clock in the brain, a structure of about 20,000 nerve cells, called the suprachiasmatic nucleus (SCN), that is found in the hypothalamus, a very clever, complex control centre. Our eyes detect changes in our environment, like light and darkness, the optic nerves in the eyes pass on this information to the brain, which then sends signals to various cells to make you feel awake or sleepy. It is the morning sunlight that stimulates a pigment in the eye called melanopsin, which signals the master clock in the brain. This helps to synchronise all body clocks to be in tune with the rhythms of Nature. Signals are sent to the pineal gland, to stop the production of melatonin, the sleep hormone, and to the adrenal gland to stimulate the production of the hormone, cortisol, the wake-up hormone (it is also the called the stress hormone since it is over-produced during times of stress).

In his book *The Darkness Manifesto – How Light Pollution Threatens the Ancient Rhythms of Life* (2022), Johan Eklöf explains this in more detail:

"As soon as our retinas are hit by the morning's Sun, photons cause signals to be sent via the nerves to the suprachiasmatic nucleus, a junction of the brain that is the centre of the circadian rhythm. From here, among other things, the pineal gland, which is responsible for the body's sleep hormone, melatonin, is controlled".

"Day light keeps the levels of melatonin at a low level, and we feel active and alert. When natural outdoor light decreases and changes colour, the amount of melatonin increases".

Johan Eklöf PhD is a Swedish bat scientist, who discovered that when lighting was introduced to old churches where bats were living, their existence was threatened because of disruption of their circadian rhythm. Most bats are nocturnal animals that need the dark to hide from predators and to feed on the insects that are active during the night. The artificial light would keep them from feeding as they would think it was daytime.

Johan's book is a must-read for everyone who is interested in Nature and the health of our planet. As mentioned in the title, light pollution - something we are very good at on our planet - is threatening the rhythms of life. From space Earth looks like a big beacon of light.

Circadian Rhythms and Health

Our circadian rhythms are closely linked to Nature's light-dark cycle, and any changes that happen in our body or in our environment can have repercussions for our health.

A good example is light exposure in the evening. Imagine spending the evening at your desk, staring at a screen and the blue light that is emitted from your computer. Of course, the phone must be checked every now and then too, so there is even more exposure to blue light. We are disturbing our circadian rhythm by telling our body it is day because of the light exposure and we are disturbing the natural wave of melatonin, that should be increasing at this time of the day and making us feel sleepy. Melatonin triggers leptin, the hormone that tells us when we feel full after eating. Low melatonin means low leptin and thus we get hungry when we shouldn't and we are tempted to have the evening munchies. Even if we went to bed at our usual time, we wouldn't be able to get to sleep easily, because we are still too alert and awake. If sleep problems keep occurring, this could have a negative impact on our health, causing chronic stress, obesity, mental health problems, etc.

Circadian rhythm disruptors are not just blue light exposure, shift work and jet lag. Genetic disorders can cause changes in genes that negatively affect our body clocks too.

And then there is another disruptor that affects us all, wherever we live in the world: Daylight-Saving Time (DST). Although the idea of Daylight-Saving Time was introduced by William Willett in the UK in 1907, it took until 1916 to be realised. Moving the clock forwards by one hour in spring and backwards by one hour in autumn creates a gap between our natural body clock and the external clocks and timings that control our lives.

In her book *Chasing the Sun* (2019), author Linda Geddes describes how the Amish people in the USA (who try to stay off the public grid) wake up about 2 hours earlier than the Americans who have free access to electricity. Their circadian rhythm is much more in tune with the natural light-dark cycle.

Another lovely example of being in tune with Nature is something Linda wrote about Buddhist monks. It is said that when monks would hold their hands up to the sun in the morning and they could see their veins, it was time for them to get up.

If you're interested in the science of sunlight and how it affects our bodies and minds, I would highly recommend this book, as it is fascinating and easy to read.

Earth's Rhythm

Rhythms are natural to our planet.

Planet Earth goes around the Sun in 365 days, 5 hours, 59 minutes, and 16 seconds to be precise, according to NASA, but Earth also rotates on its own axis, giving us a 24-hour day.

Within the 24-hour day we have a Sunrise in the morning and a Sunset in the evening, creating a day and night/light and dark cycle.

The Moon circles around Earth in about a month and it takes the same amount of time for the Moon to rotate on its own axis, just like Earth does. Everyone on Earth can see the same Moon, but from different angles. Moon-phases are caused by the fact the Moon is always half-lit by the Sun. One side of the Moon catches the reflected Sunlight, the other side, that is facing away, is in the dark. Moonlight is in fact reflected Sunlight.

While the Moon goes around Earth, the Sun shines its light on different sides and what part of the Moon catches this reflected Sunlight defines the lunar phase.

There are 8 lunar phases:

- New Moon, which we can't see from Earth, the Sun is behind the Moon
- Waxing Crescent (increasing Sunlight on the Moon)
- First Quarter
- Waxing Gibbous
- Full Moon, the Sun shines her light on the side of the Moon that is facing us.
- Waning Gibbous (decreasing Sunlight on the Moon)
- Last Quarter
- Waning Crescent

Tides

Having lived near the sea in the Netherlands and visiting the Cornish coast in England every year, I have always been intrigued by the tides. What is it that makes the water move?

Tides are the regular rise and fall of sea levels, that are caused by the gravitational pull of the Sun and the Moon on our rotating Earth. Physics was never my strongest subject at school, so I won't go into further detail about why this happens, but it's a given fact, one of the fabulous rhythms in Nature, that I find fascinating to watch.

In the UK there are two high tides and two low tides every day, but the height of these tides is not always the same, it varies according to the phase of the Moon. If it is Full Moon or New Moon the gravitational pull is at its strongest as Earth, Sun and Moon are aligned. At these times the difference between low and high tide is the greatest, this is called Spring Tide. When the difference between low and high tide is the smallest (Moon in first or third quarter) it is called Neap Tide.

Tides are occurring in a natural rhythm and animals that live on the coastal land bordering the sea or ocean often show biological rhythms that are in tune with the tidal cycles. The way these animals function and behave is controlled in harmony with the tidal cycle, a tidally-adapted rhythm originating from within the animals.

Seasons

Seasons are another element of Nature's rhythm. The reason why we have seasons is because Earth's axis is somewhat slanted in relation to its course around the Sun, which means that some areas of Earth get more solar energy than others. This has an effect on temperatures and what is happening in Nature. When we are experiencing winter in the UK, the Australians are having BBQs on the beach, because the Northern and Southern Hemispheres have opposite seasons.

Astronomical seasons are marked by equinoxes (when day and night are almost the same length) and solstices (the longest and shortest days).

In the Northern Hemisphere, where we are, the spring equinox takes place in March, the summer solstice is in June, the autumn equinox is in September and the winter solstice is in December. The start of the equinoxes and solstices varies slightly every year, so the astronomical seasons vary annually. For example, the Spring equinox happens sometime between 19 March and 21 March.

Meteorological seasons are a little more straightforward, as they are marked by temperature trends and divided into four seasons of 3 months each. In the Northern Hemisphere winter starts on 1 December, spring on 1 March, summer on 1 June and autumn on 1 September.

No matter which of these approaches you choose to define the seasons, you will be able to know when it is winter, spring, summer, or autumn when you observe the natural rhythms and cycles of the world around you; it's the beauty of being in tune with Nature. Watching the leaves change colour and fall from the trees, seeing the first snowdrops popping up or the Helleborus flowering, butterflies fluttering and the delicate smell of honeysuckle, migrating birds and hawthorn berries on bare branches, are all signs of changing seasons.

Winter Blues

You have probably heard of 'Winter Blues' or Seasonal Affective Disorder (SAD) and maybe even you or someone you know suffers from it. About 5% of people suffer from SAD each year, a seasonal depression that, although the exact cause is not known, has been linked to reduced exposure to sunlight during the winter. I wouldn't say I suffer from SAD myself, but the dark and gloomy days in winter definitely affect my mood adversely.

As we have seen before, our circadian rhythms are closely linked to Nature's light-dark cycle. In winter there is less sunlight, the days are shorter, we spend more time indoors, and if there is not enough daylight exposure this could disrupt our body clock and cause symptoms of SAD such as feeling low, lacking energy, feeling gloomy and listless, just wanting to sleep, craving carbohydrates, and gaining weight.

The disrupted body clock affects the hypothalamus, our sophisticated control centre, causing higher levels of melatonin (making us sleepy) and lower levels of serotonin (our 'happy hormone'). A daylight lamp or SAD lamp does work well, but has to be used every day during the darker periods.

Not totally surprising, there is also something called 'Summer Blues' or Reversed SAD.

In this case the longer days, longer hours of sunlight and shorter nights can trigger problems. Summer SAD, just like the winter variant, is related to various factors, but the most important one seems to be hormonal changes affecting the daily circadian rhythm, like overproduction of melatonin and the change in serotonin, the hormone that regulates mood.

Body temperature, which is also part of our circadian rhythm, can also have an effect. Normally our body temperature drops when we sleep, but if it is hot in summer, it could go up and keep us awake. When your circadian rhythm is disrupted, we can no longer adjust to the seasonal changes in the length of the day.

Just like the 'Winter Blues' sleep disturbances are a characteristic of Summer SAD. Other symptoms are lack of energy, low mood, insomnia, and anxiety.

In Part Two, 'Nature & Nutrition, we will look, amongst other things, at seasonal eating and how biodynamic farmers watch the rhythms and cycles of the earth, sun, moon, stars, and planets and the effects these have on the growth and development of their produce.

> *"We trust nature to know what it is doing, but we are not nearly so kind, understanding and trusting of our own rhythms and cycles. It's ridiculous that we are so hard on ourselves. Can we not trust that the very same forces that created the rhythms and cycles of nature created our own? Of course, we can. We often don't, but we can, if we remember."*
> Jeffrey R. Anderson, *The Nature of Things -*
> *Navigating Everyday Life with Grace*
> *Religious Science minister and teacher of New Thought / Ancient Wisdom*

OUR CONNECTION WITH NATURE

Humans and Nature are both part of one connected system, both following the natural rhythms that dominate our planet. The idea that the natural rhythms are there is reassuring for all living creatures, knowing that after night there is day, after winter there is spring to look forward to, etc.

The 18th century German scientist and explorer, Alexander von Humboldt, who is often called 'The Forgotten Father of Environmentalism', described Nature as a part of one interconnected organism, Earth, where everything from microbes to human beings, has its part to play, and that doesn't exist only for the use of humans.

In *Psychopathology of the Human-Nature Relationship,* the American psychologist and researcher Ralph Metzner, gives us another interesting analogy of our connection with Nature: "We are part of nature; we are *in* the Earth, not on it. We are like the cells in the body of the vast living organism that is planet Earth. An organism cannot continue to function healthily if one group of cells decides to dominate and cannibalize the other energy systems of the body". If everyone saw their connection with Nature like this, wouldn't we be in a much better place? Looking after the planet like you're looking after your own body, with care and respect, and finding a balance so that humans and Nature can both thrive.

There are many theories about the human relationship with Nature, but one that stands out is the 'Biophilia' theory; biophilia meaning a love of life and all living things. It was first introduced by the German American psychoanalyst Erich Fromm in his book, *The Anatomy of Human Destructiveness* (1973). The term popped up again in the American biologist Edward O. Wilson's book *Biophilia* (1984) in which he suggested that 'Biophilia' is partially in our genes. When you think about the millions of years of evolution and the close human relationship with other living organisms that has always existed, the suggestion that we are genetically attracted to Nature makes sense.

Are you scared of snakes or spiders? Do you get frightened when there is thunder and lightning and you have no idea where this fear is coming from? There is an interesting connection with the Biophilia theory here that could be seen as evidence for the genetic connection between us and Nature. Think back to our ancestors, who were living in Nature, not well-protected in houses, continually exposed to predators, snakes, spiders, toxic plants, natural phenomena, etc. Their fear meant that they were conscious of the danger and had a chance of survival and it is this fear that has been passed on through evolution.

Another theory on why we are attracted and want to be connected with Nature is called the 'Savanna Hypothesis' (proposed by Gordon Orians in 1980, 1986). Our hunter-gatherer ancestors moved from the forests to the savanna, a type of landscape that gave them everything for survival: food, trees among which to hide from their predators and stay protected from the elements, and wide views so they could predate and catch prey much more easily. The trees growing on the savanna, like the acacia tree, had spreading canopies and research in the 1980s showed that these trees are still preferred by people nowadays, a preference that probably originates in an innate knowing of the habitat in which it's best to live. Our responses to Nature are universal.

To me there is nothing more interesting than putting a theory into practice. As luck would have it, I recently travelled to South Africa and experienced the Karoo, the semi-desert area, and a bit of the savanna. According to the Savanna Hypothesis we should be attracted to the landscape and feel strong emotions since the savanna has been hugely important in the development of modern human beings. I have to say that looking at the vast shrubland and trees was overwhelming, possibly because I was trying to picture our ancestors there, but also because to me it was natural beauty.

What is interesting is that studies on human reactions to Nature show that we respond more positively to trees than to other plant types, and that the more contact we have with Nature when we are youngsters, the more positive our feelings are towards trees as grown-ups. Tree colours are all experienced as soothing, but the bright green colour wins first prize here, as it is associated with healthy plants that would potentially be good for our survival.

Something completely different in this context is a phenomenon that I stumbled upon purely by accident. I was cracking some walnuts for a cake

I was making and looking at the walnuts, they reminded me of the human brain, because of the shape and patterns. Ever the curious cat, I did a bit of digging and I found out about 'fractals'.

Fractals are repeating patterns that are identical or alike, found in Nature, such as flowers, snowflakes, ocean waves, etc. Think of a tree and how the big branches form a pattern, with smaller branches coming off them, and this pattern repeating itself until we get to the leaves, that have veins with the same pattern. Taking this a bit further, looking at a picture of our lungs, do they remind you of something?

Lungs look like upside down trees, with bronchi, bronchioles and alveoli resembling the branches, twigs, and leaves. Trees and lungs share an important function: breathing. Just like us, trees breathe. Human beings inhale oxygen and exhale carbon dioxide, trees do the opposite as their leaves absorb carbon dioxide and through photosynthesis, they produce oxygen.

Fractals expert, Richard Taylor, a physicist at the University of Oregon, describes fractals as Nature's basic building blocks. He has also done a lot of research on the effect of fractals on human health and found that, just by looking at fractals, stress levels went down as much as 60%. Interestingly, people don't have to be in Nature itself to reduce their stress, looking at Nature scenes on the computer produces a similar effect. So, get yourself a fractal screensaver on your computer, or even better, go out and look at the trees!

You're probably asking yourself how this stress reduction is possible, as it is pretty amazing. Well, our ancestors are in the picture again here, as they were looking at fractal patterns in Nature all the time and processed what they saw very fast. Our brain has evolved to respond positively to fractals, and very quickly, it only takes 50 milliseconds to detect the presence of fractals and feel in your comfort zone. Fractals bring calm and a sense of belonging.

So, we have established that we are all part of Nature, following the natural rhythms, and that we have a tendency to find connections with Nature and all living things. Once this balance is disrupted, it has negative effects on our health, but what positive effects does Nature have on us and will we be able to restore the balance if we have lost the connection?

FOREST BATHING

When I once mentioned 'Forest Bathing' to a friend, she thought I was talking about 'tree hugging'. While you can certainly hug a tree when you're Forest Bathing, it is a lot more than that. Looking into the research on this Nature therapy, I was amazed by the number of studies that have been done, especially in Asia.

One of the people I interviewed for this book is Thinley Om, a Bhutanese Traditional Medicine Practitioner. You can read Thinley's story in Part Three, the conversations, but I would like to mention her passion for Forest Bathing here, and share some of the research she has done.

According to Thinley, Forest Bathing is simply being calm and quiet amongst the trees, observing Nature around you, whilst breathing deeply. It is not just for the serious meditator or wilderness-lover, it can be practiced by walking in any natural environment, where you are consciously connecting with what is around you. Research has shown that Forest Bathing is beneficial for physical and mental wellbeing, but Thinley adds that it also helps us to develop kindness and compassion for all living things and increases self-love. In Bhutan one can join a trained guide for a meditative 2–3-hour Forest Bathing or ecotherapy session. Other countries offer this possibility as well, for those who don't like to do it by themselves and prefer a more structured experience.

In the 1980s, the term Forest Bathing or 'Shinrin-yoku' emerged in Japan. It is referring to a healing technique that brings back physical and psychological health through a 'five senses experience' (seeing, smelling, hearing, touching, and tasting), while exposing the body to a forest environment, mindfully engaging with Nature.

In South Korea the first therapeutic forest was opened in 2009 by the Korea Forest Service. By 2020 there were 32 of these forests, with 1.5 million visitors, despite the Covid pandemic. The Forest Service considers phytoncides (tree essentials oils), sounds, sunlight, anions (negatively charged ions, found just about everywhere, released by trees) and oxygen levels to be the healing factors in the forest, and they use different therapeutic approaches, such as walking and spending time in the forest, walking in a valley and immersing your limbs in water, drinking tea, meditation, and exercise.

A scientific review of Japanese publications on Forest Bathing done by researchers of Chiba University in Japan (2016) found that natural stimuli help to reduce stress and strengthen our immune system. The studies they reviewed showed lower salivary cortisol (one of our stress hormones), lower blood pressure, lower pulse rate, lower blood sugar levels and improvement in Natural Killer Cell (NKC) activity, which enhances the immune system.

Natural Killer Cells are immune cells that are our early defence against infections as they kill virally infected cells. They also detect and control early signs of cancer.

A series of studies done in Japan over a number of years, investigating the effect of Forest Bathing on the immune system specifically, showed that a three-day trip to the forest increased Natural Killer Cell activity, but not only that, the increased level of NKCs lasted for more than a month! It turns out that it is the phytoncides (essential oils) released from trees that increase NKC activity. Phytoncides also work on our central nervous system and have soothing qualities as they reduce the level of cortisol.

Mental health impacts of Forest Bathing were researched in the UK, by the University of Derby (2020). Researchers found that Forest Bathing can be effective in reducing mental health symptoms in the short term, especially anxiety.

The first study on Forest Bathing in the UK appeared in the 'Sustainability' journal in January 2021. This study, that was conducted by 7 different organisations including the Forest Bathing Institute, reported major improvements in mental problems such as depression, anger and confusion. There was more connection with Nature, people felt more 'pro-environment' and had more compassion for themselves and others.

Forestry England cares for over 1,500 of our nation's forests and they shape landscapes for people, wildlife, and timber. To help people find a way to connect with forests to support their wellbeing, Forestry England has been supporting Social Prescribing Day in March 2023.

Social prescribing is a way of connecting people to non-medical activities, groups, and support to meet the practical, social, and emotional needs that affect their health and wellbeing. Sometimes doctors and medicine are not able to treat people as people's health and wellbeing are determined mostly by a whole range of social, economic, and environmental factors. Forest Bathing makes an excellent activity to be socially prescribed.

If you are interested in Forest Bathing and you would like to experience a guided session, check out the Forest Bathing Institute; they run Forest Bathing sessions all over the UK.

https://tfb.institute/

MENTAL HEALTH

When I was a student in the Netherlands, I struggled with anxiety and depression, but in those days, there wasn't much support available, hence I had to find my own way to deal with it. After a while I realised that being in Nature made me feel better, so whenever I felt down or anxious, I would take my bicycle and go for a ride through the polder. Now for those who don't know what a polder is, it is a piece of lowland that is reclaimed from the sea or inland water and is surrounded by dikes. Cycling on my own over the dikes, in the open space, exposed to the elements and surrounded by green fields, calmed me immensely.

I also spent time with my parents in France, where they had bought a derelict farmhouse in the unspoilt countryside of the Alliers. Being surrounded by Nature improved my mental health and the times I stayed there were magical, as I had never been as close to Nature anywhere else. There were trees and fields everywhere, wildflowers, hedgerows, wildlife, lots of gardening, the slow pace of the countryside and no light pollution.

So, what was it in Nature that improved my mental wellbeing?

As mentioned before, trees release phytoncides that decrease the production of cortisol, but there is much more. And of course, it could be the fractals that I was seeing in Nature that provided me with a feeling of calm and a sense of belonging.

Or was it the genetic attraction as described in the 'Biophilia' theory? After all, I was living in the city in a high-rise apartment, surrounded by concrete, railway and roads, with the polder being my bit of Nature to which I could escape.

In 2020, researchers of the Chungbuk National University in South Korea published a study that describes the healing process one goes through when exposed to Nature in six different steps. They came to these steps after analysing 180 essays on forest therapy experiences from people with various physiological, mental, and social problems (like loneliness or unemployment), men and women, ranging in age from teenagers to seniors in their 80s.

The first step is stimulation. Nature stimulates all our senses: think of the smell of a pine tree, or freshly cut grass, the sound of an owl, the taste of a ripe blackberry freshly picked from the hedgerow, the view of a wildflower meadow, I could go on.... I don't know about you, but these things make me feel happy.

The next step is acceptance. Nature makes people feel as if they can be themselves; Nature doesn't judge.

Step 3 is the purification stage, where there is a release of negativity. You can scream and shout, cry and vent your negative energy, tell the trees your problems and Nature will listen and won't judge.

While walking through Nature, there is time for awareness and self-reflection, and you often experience clarity on how to move on. It is the stage of insight when the penny drops.

Recharging is the next step, where Nature gives people hope and the will to live and fills them with positive energy.

The final step is change. After being recharged with positive energy, people have the will to change what needs to be addressed in their lives so there could be healing and recovery.

STRESS

Stress is often a cause of mental health problems, especially when it is chronic stress.

Where you live is influential too, as living in an urban environment is more stressful than living in a rural environment and although there are benefits to living in the city, there are also risks of mental health problems. This is quite worrying given that about 56% of the world's population is living in cities today, and this percentage will only go up.

Studies have shown that the amygdala, the part of the brain involved in processing stress and emotions, is less activated during stress in people living in rural areas compared to people living in the city.

There is a correlation between the amount of green space in people's living environment and their general health, hence it is extremely important that there are accessible natural areas in these urban environments, so people have a chance to get out and experience the benefits of Nature. Research has shown that the stress recovery rate was much higher in people exposed to Nature, than in those who were exposed to an urban environment.

The botanist James Wong, who was filming in Singapore, recently posted on Instagram that in Singapore, the most biodiverse capital city of the world, 50% of the city is now green space and that they have the intention of planting 1 million more tress by 2030! This is amazing given that Singapore lost 99% of its original forest cover during the colonial period. And it is not just the Botanical Gardens that create the green space, but buildings, car parks, sky gardens, it's everywhere. Especially worth mentioning is the Khoo Teck Phuat Hospital that is totally covered in vegetation.

Research has shown that patients whose hospital room looks out on a natural scene have shorter postoperative hospital stays than those patients who have a room with windows facing the walls of a building. Having plants in the hospital room itself seems to have a positive effect as well.

We often don't have a choice about where we live, but there is always a way to find some green space for an outdoor activity, even if it is a small park.

A NEW HOBBY

I would like to tell you a bit about my husband, a serious workaholic, who certainly didn't get his work-life balance right, with the usual consequences.

I kept telling him to get a hobby, but like with all life changes, the person in question will have to make the first move. Eventually he made up his mind and announced he wanted to keep bees, starting off with doing the courses and putting two beehives in the back garden. Fast-forward eight years and he has 20 beehives in three different semi-rural locations, is a member of two beekeeping associations, wins prizes with his honey and honeycomb and mentors new beekeepers, but most of all, he spends a lot time outdoors in Nature, working with these amazing creatures. He absolutely loves it and he schedules his beekeeping in his diary to make sure he makes time for it. I sometimes wonder who he loves more, me or the bees…

Why am I telling you this? It is an example of how one can improve health by opting for an outdoor activity, being close to Nature.

THERAPEUTIC GARDENING

Using gardening as a physical and mental health intervention is becoming more popular these days. Gardening can transform lives. Physical activity, being outdoors, connecting with others, learning new skills, and having a sense of achievement and purpose all have beneficial effects on our health.

One of the people I interviewed for this book is Tone Tellefsen-Hughes, who founded the Green Hub Project for Teens in 2021. In the garden behind her practice, the project offers Nature-based therapy for teenagers who are struggling with stress, anxiety, and depression.

I was very pleased to be able to talk to one of the first teenagers who joined the project, Abby, to learn more about the benefits of Nature and gardening on the mind, and how it supported her own wellbeing. You can read Tone and Abby's stories in Part Three.

GREEN SOCIAL PRESCRIBING PROGRAMMES

Having mentioned social prescribing before, I would very much like to highlight a wonderful example of nature-based green social prescribing.

I happened to meet Dr Lucy Loveday at the Integrative & Personalised

Medicine Congress in London, where she was giving a talk with the title 'Exploring possibility – A future with nature at the heart of health for all'.

Apart from being a General Practitioner and an experienced educator, Lucy is the founder of 'Resilient Young Minds', a nature-based green social prescribing programme for 18–25-year-olds in Devon, UK. It is a programme for marginalised and disadvantaged young people, who are socially isolated and/or suffer with mental health issues. It is an opportunity for them to learn more about how nature can support their wellbeing and embark on a supported transformational journey to personal and environmental wellbeing.

All interactive sessions are run by Lucy and an experienced woodland tutor.

There is a whole host of activities offered, including art, photography and fire lighting, and participants learn about mindfulness, movement, connection, conservation, etc. This programme will also help these young people to gain confidence and feel a sense of belonging. The programme, that took place in November and December 2022, was successful: 75% of the participants reported an improvement in mental wellbeing and a staggering 92% reported to feel more connected to nature.

In 2022 Resilient Young Minds won the Health Equity Innovation Award (South West Academic Health Science Network). This enabled the programme to be rigorously evaluated with a mixed methods approach. In Autumn 2023 Resilient Young Minds will pilot a 'Train the Trainer' model within the education sector for 11-16 year olds and Lucy's vision is that all children & young people experiencing disadvantage have equal opportunities to access and experience nature for wellbeing.

Let's hope that initiatives like this can be rolled out to the rest of the country, as there is without doubt a need for it.

PART TWO

NATURE & NUTRITION

'Live in each season as it passes; breathe the air, drink the drink, taste the fruit, and resign yourself to the influence of the earth.'

Henry David Thoreau
American naturalist, essayist, poet, and philosopher

Nature provides us with all the nutrients we need to survive and thrive: fruits, vegetables, legumes, wholegrains, nuts, seeds, meat, fish, etc. This is why we should make an effort to eat as Nature intends and try to stay clear of processed foods. Eating 'manufactured' foods is one of the causes of our disconnection from Nature (and a source of health problems). Not knowing where your food comes from is another reason that we feel disconnected.

Photo by Kerry J https://kerryjphotography.co.uk/

Looking at the connection between Nature and nutrition from a different angle, I stumbled upon a study, that was conducted among 317 adults in Philadelphia, to research the relationship between feeling connected to Nature, or Nature relatedness, and dietary behaviours, including dietary diversity and fruit and vegetable intake. The result of the study was that people who are more connected with Nature were more likely to have a healthy diet, including more variety of foods and a higher fruit and vegetable intake.

In this chapter I would like to introduce you to some other interesting aspects of the link between Nature and nutrition.

FOOD WASTE

Nature has always provided us with everything we need to survive, and thrive, and one of those gifts is food. In my view wasting food is disrespectful to Nature and morally wrong, given the number of people affected by hunger in the world, which increased to as many as 828 million in 2021. I still remember my mother reminding me of the hungry children elsewhere in the world, when I didn't empty my plate. To me it was surreal then, until I was older and started travelling and witnessed poverty and hunger in parts of Asia, India, and Africa. Experiences like that leave a mark on your soul and we try to reduce food waste as much as we can.

We buy food and eat it, but do we ever think about what is involved in getting that food on our plate? Not just how it was cooked, but also how it was grown, how the animals were fed, what production methods were used and how it was transported? Most of us are probably more focused on getting the items on our shopping lists and what we are going to do with the food. But there is a lot more to food than shopping and cooking. Think about food waste for instance.

How careful are you to put all your cooked and uncooked waste in the food recycling bin? Do you know what happens to the contents of the food caddy that is collected by many Councils every week?

The Environment Act 2021 became law in November 2021, introducing changes to waste collection so that recyclable household waste (which includes food waste) must be 'collected separately from other household waste'. The government has made the commitment to roll out separate weekly household food waste collection across England by 2023.

The weekly food waste collection takes your food waste to an anaerobic digestion facility, where micro-organisms break down the food waste, producing biogas which is collected and used to generate electricity, heat, and transport fuel. It also creates biofertiliser that can be used in farming and land regeneration.

Every bit of food you put in the caddy actually produces real energy and whilst it would be better to have no food waste, at least it is used for a good purpose.

So how much food do we waste?

Well, in the UK, we throw away around 9.5 million tonnes of food and drink every year, the majority of which could have been used. It is estimated that one in five bags of food shopping goes to waste each week. On a global scale around 17% of global food production may go wasted, according to the UN Environment Programme's Food Waste Index Report 2021, with 61% of this waste coming from households, 27% from food service and 13% from retail. These shocking amounts of food waste are taxing on the food waste management systems, they increase food insecurity, and they have a major effect on global climate change, biodiversity and pollution.

Globally, according to the Food and Agriculture Organisation of the United Nations (FAO), one in nine people are suffering from chronic malnutrition. Malnutrition is not just because of lack of food, it can also be caused by too much of the wrong food, leading to obesity and related complications such as diabetes and heart disease. With an expected increase of the world's population to more than 9 billion by 2050, it is no surprise that there is a critical issue on how all the world's inhabitants will be able to feed themselves.

It is difficult to tell exactly where the food is wasted, but it is not just the consumer who is the culprit, although research has shown that households are to blame for the largest amount of waste in the UK. Food producers, i.e., farmers and growers, food manufacturers, retailers, restaurants, hotels, etc. make up the rest.

Fortunately, there is now the realisation that the challenge the world is facing is monumental, and that we cannot go on like this. A government briefing paper on food waste (August 2016) states, "If food waste cannot be prevented then the waste hierarchy would then support first the redistribution of surplus food to humans, and if not suitable for that purpose, then used for animal feed (under strict conditions) …". A great example of this is the supermarket TESCO that works with Fareshare (the UK's largest charity fighting hunger and food waste), to donate surplus food from its stores to local charities and community groups.

Each week our organic vegetable supplier now offers a Zero Waste Surprise Bag that will contain three different items of organic fruit, veg, salad, or herbs. They can't tell you what you'll get; contents change day by day to use what's fresh and plentiful. Contents shift with the seasons, bringing you whatever is overflowing from their fields and grower friends.

Another initiative to reduce food waste is the App 'Too Good To Go', which let restaurants, bakeries, etc. list what food they have left over. This food can then be bought via the App with a big discount and collected before the store closes.

Reducing food waste is just one aspect of the challenge to the food system that we face. Food is also at the core of many environmental concerns – it's a major contributor to climate change and responsible for 60% global biodiversity loss.

The British Nutrition Foundation describes the questions that will need to be answered as follows:

"How can we achieve a dietary pattern that provides us with the many nutrients we need for health, in appropriate amounts, but that is also equitable, affordable, and sustainable? And how do we produce more food with fewer resources, such as land, water, and fuel, to feed the growing global population?"

There are no easy answers to the questions and the fact that there are so many parties involved doesn't make it any easier.

What can we as consumers do?

- Reduce food waste.
- Shop smart and use a shopping list based on your meal plans.
- Freeze or use leftovers (great for next day's lunch).
- Make less food or try to estimate portion sizes more accurately.
- Use smaller plates.
- Mindful eating makes you eat less, as you eat slower, and you will feel full more quickly.
- Tidy up your food cupboard, fridge, and freezer so you know what's there.
- Order less food when eating out or ask for a doggy bag.
- Store food properly so it won't go off so quickly.
- Buy loose food items instead of prepacked food.
- Don't fall for 'bargains' in the supermarket that make you buy more than you need.
- Get a compost bin or use the food bin supplied by the local authorities.

- Eat a balanced, varied diet with foods from all food groups (protein-rich foods – animal or plant-based, vegetables and fruit, healthy fats, carbohydrates).
- Make vegetables and fruit a bigger part of your diet.
- Buy local, seasonal foods where possible.
- Eat less meat, especially red meat.

These steps may not seem much, but the total of every individual's actions can have a huge effect. Every step counts.

Gleaning

"And when ye reap the harvest of your land, thou shalt not make clean riddance of the corners of thy field when thou reapest, neither shalt thou gather any gleaning of thy harvest: thou shalt leave them unto the poor, and to the stranger" - Leviticus xxiii, 22.

The above Bible text shows that gleaning is a very old practice. If you want to know what gleaning used to look like in the olden days, google Jean-François Millet, The Gleaners. Millet completed this oil painting that is also called Des glaneuse, in 1857. It portrays three peasant women, who are gleaning a field of wheat. If you would like to admire the original painting, it is now hanging in the Musée d'Orsay in Paris.

Nowadays gleaning is practised by charity groups that distribute the gleaned food to those in need; in a modern setting, this can be food collection from supermarkets that would otherwise throw away food at the end of the day, or picking up food from farmers, who donate surplus produce or produce that is wonky, that doesn't meet the requirements for the retailers or that has been left in their fields, to donate to local food banks, charities and food projects.

Gleaning is a way of saving food, food recovery, and putting it to good use. It won't resolve the problem of food waste or food insecurity completely, but it gives people an idea of the food system and it does make a difference. In the UK The Gleaning Network is a network of groups, organisations, farmers, charities, and enthusiastic volunteers who are all working to reduce farm-level food waste. Gleaning is a good way for people to connect with each other and learn about our food system.

GROWING YOUR OWN FOOD

If you are fortunate enough to have a garden with enough space to grow some fruit and vegetables, I would highly recommend it. There is nothing more rewarding than picking some fresh produce and eating it. I still get excited when I can pick the first sun-ripened tomatoes and make a tomato salad or soup. The fun starts with planning what you are going to grow, getting the seeds or seedlings, planting and nurturing the plants.

Besides the harvesting, cooking with the freshest ingredients and eating the final product, all the hard work that precedes that is a journey that will bring you closer to Nature, with your hands in the soil and the sun on your face, although the last one is not always guaranteed of course. I still get bowled over by the beauty, resilience, and force of Nature. Like the tomato plants that appeared on our compost heap, after we had thrown a few manky, green tomatoes away in early autumn. Wasteful, I know, but we really don't like green tomato chutney, and, in the end, they were useful for the plants that appeared. Nature surprises me time and time again.

But even if you don't have a garden, there are still ways to grow your own food.

You can grow many different foods such as tomatoes, cucumbers, beans, courgettes, herbs, etc. in pots, big or small, on patios, window ledges and balconies.

Growing your own food is not difficult. At its most basic, growing food is simply a matter of putting seeds into decent, healthy soil, watering it, and watching it grow. It also has environmental benefits. Your home-grown vegetables and fruit won't be packed in plastic; by eating home-grown vegetables you will be reducing your carbon footprint as many vegetables from the supermarket were grown a long distance away, and less pesticides will be used if you decide to grow your own.

All very positive effects on our environment, but let's not forget the personal benefits of growing your own food. Firstly, you have easy access to fresh, seasonally, hopefully organic vegetables and fruit. Another, almost more important benefit in my view, and I'm sure many parents of young children will agree with me, is the effect that 'growing your own food' has on children's eating behaviour if you let them participate in the gardening.

We all know a little fussy eater who doesn't eat many vegetables and no matter what we try, the behaviour won't change. NHS data (Health Survey for England) show that in the UK in 2018 only 18% of children between 5 and 15 years old consumed the recommended five or more portions of fruit and vegetables, and over 10% of the children in this age group ate less than one portion a day!

But there is hope… A study conducted in 2020 by the Konkuk University in Seoul, showed that when children plant, grow, and harvest vegetables themselves, their aversion to vegetables reduced and their preference for and understanding of different types of foods increased. As a result, the children started to eat more vegetables. Educating children in nutrition and giving them cookery lessons will improve the eating attitudes to vegetables even more. Having had the experience of a school allotment myself, and in my role as a nutritional therapist, I fully agree on this.

The other option is to join an allotment association or a community garden.

It is wonderful to be able to experience the seasons, learn about the ecosystem and become more environmentally aware. And it is of course also a great way to meet like-minded people and make new friends.

Photo by Kerry J https://kerryjphotography.co.uk/

Community Gardens and Allotments

In 2017 the University of Sao Paulo, Brazil, published a research paper on 'the impact of urban gardens on adequate and healthy foods'.

We all know that eating fruit and vegetables has great health benefits, but what specific effects does growing your own produce have on people who are participating in a community garden project in an urban environment?

Apart from being able to grow and eat organic fruit and vegetables, and reduce food costs, the urban community garden also teaches people the importance of healthy eating, and the research showed that many participants developed an interest in cooking and meal planning, which to me is crucial for a healthy lifestyle. Sharing food with others and working together as a group in the garden brings the community together. Being outdoors, in touch with the soil and growing your own produce connects people with Nature, which, as described in Part One, has valuable physical and mental health benefits.

An interesting example in the UK is the Sutton Community Farm in South London. This peri-urban farm on the outskirts of London was originally set up in 2010 by two local environmental charities, BioRegional and EcoLocal, with the aim of teaching local people about growing food, advocating health and wellbeing, bringing the community together and boosting the supply of local food products. Since 2013 the farm is legally owned by the community and has grown into a business that produces more than fifteen tonnes of fresh vegetables a year and offers a weekly vegetable box scheme, all done with the help of up to eighty volunteers.

More recently, in November 2022, Hounslow Council announced a new policy, 'Grow for the Future'. Hounslow is a large suburban district of West London.

This policy will give local communities the chance to grow food and teach children about healthy living. About 27 acres of unused land throughout the borough will be turned into community gardens, allotments, and orchards.

Each new site will be linked to a local school for educational purposes such as teaching urban children about nutrition, healthy living, and the origin of their food. The food that these schools will be growing on the sites will be given to school children and their families to help reduce food bills and put food on their plates. What a great initiative.

Community gardens and allotments are not the same thing.

My husband and I are members of a local Allotment Association, and we have an individual plot of land where we grow fruit and vegetables. It is not a community garden as everyone works on their own allotment and takes their harvest home. There was a glimmer of hope though this year, when one of the members suggested collecting surplus fruit and vegetables to donate to the local food bank. It turned out to be quite a successful venture.

Allotments have been around for hundreds of years, but the allotments, as we know them today, emerged in the 1800s, when land was given to the poor to grow their own food, which was much needed, given the negative effects of the Industrial Revolution (low wages, poor living and working conditions) and the lack of a welfare state.

In 1908 the Small Holdings and Allotments Act was introduced, and local authorities had to provide adequate allotments. In England, it wasn't until the end of World War I that allotments were made available to everyone, mainly to help the service men that returned from war. There was extensive use of allotments during and after World War II.

Local authorities are required to develop a food growing strategy for their area, which includes the allocation of land for possible allotment sites, but also sites for the community where they can grow vegetables, fruit, herbs, or flowers.

CHRONONUTRITION

I bet you noticed a difference in your daily routine during the Covid pandemic. No commutes, getting up later, shifting breakfast time, less exercise, just to name a few changes.

The number of clients I saw after the pandemic with weight problems and sleep issues is a good indicator that these changes in the daily routine had had a negative effect on their metabolism. Some of the clients hadn't eaten more than usual and had still been quite active, which was very frustrating for them, until we started talking about chrono-nutrition.

Earlier in the book I talked about natural rhythms and the circadian clock. Over the last 10 years we have learned a lot about the link between our body clocks and nutrition, as researchers linked research of biological rhythms and nutrition research, calling this new field of research 'chrono-nutrition'. So, what were the findings?

Our central body clock (suprachiasmatic nucleus, SCN) is brought into a specific rhythm by two key signals that are also called 'zeitgebers' or natural time cues: food intake and light. Food intake or eating behaviour follows a clear circadian pattern, hence the time of the day when you eat your food influences your metabolism.

A study found that women who were trying to lose weight and ate their main meal before 3pm, lost more weight than those who ate their main meal after 3pm. All women ate the same types of food, were equally active and slept for a comparable amount of time.

However, it is not just what time you eat that impacts your metabolism, digestion, and hunger. It is also about fasting, time-restricted eating and how often you eat. Blood sugar is also affected by what time of the day you eat your food. Research has found that our body's capability to control blood sugar is different throughout the day. The ZOE Predict1 study looked at this among more than 1,000 participants and they found that, on average, their blood sugar response was twice as high after eating a meal for lunch, compared to eating the same meal for breakfast. Blood sugar metabolism is affected by circadian rhythms, but of course, we have to bear in mind that everyone responds to food differently.

By the way, researchers also found out that the first meal you eat after a long fast, i.e., breakfast, is important for the synchronization of your body clock.

Timing of meals doesn't just have an impact on physical health, it may also play a role in the development of mental health issues. A 2019 study that looked at eating times and mood disorders, showed that among 1,304 people those who skipped or delayed breakfast were more likely to develop a mood disorder than those who would eat breakfast, lunch and dinner at regular times.

Chrono-nutrition studies the link between food, mealtimes, metabolism, and circadian rhythms. It is a field that needs further research, especially given the huge impact chrono-nutrition has on human physiology, disease, and the optimum wellbeing of us humans.

Light

In Part One 'Nature and Health', I wrote extensively about the light-dark cycle and how this affects our sleeping pattern. Not only is good sleep essential for our cognitive functioning, but it is also crucial for our metabolism, appetite regulation, hormone regulation and immune system. Just like food, the daily light and dark cycle is an important natural time cue that affects the circadian pattern.

HEALTHY SOIL, HEALTHY FOOD

Since the 1950s the nutritional values of certain crops have decreased quite dramatically. An American study (2004) looked at 13 different nutrients in 43 garden crops. Six nutrients (protein, calcium, iron, phosphorus, ascorbic acid, and vitamin B2) showed declines between 6% and 38%, with vitamin B2 being the nutrient that had decreased the most (38%).

The American geologist David Montgomery and his wife, biologist Anne Biklé researched soil health and how regenerative soil farming leads to healthier soil and a higher nutrient density in food.

Conventional farming disturbs the much-needed healthy relationship between the soil and the plants. Interest is growing in how farming practices affect the quality of our food.

How we treat the soil affects its mineral micronutrients (including iron, folate and zinc), phytochemicals and the fat profile of meat and dairy produce. For example, excessive use of synthetic fertilisers affects the uptake of mineral micronutrients by the plants. Plants are not taking nutrients from the soil so that we can be healthy, they are taking them up for their own benefit.

One of Montgomery and Biklé's experiments involved wheat. A wheat farmer was interested to see if he could grow similar wheat if he did not use the herbicide glyphosate on some of his fields. Although the crop yields were about the same, the big difference was in the nutrients. The more regenerative grown crop had much higher levels of nutrients. Zinc for instance was more than 50% higher! Other bigger experiments showed that on regenerative farms phytochemical levels were, on average, 20-25% higher, and some vitamins were 14-35% higher.

Soil health means human health. If you are interested in this subject, I would recommend the book Montgomery and Biklé wrote, *What Your Food Ate: How to Restore Our Land and Reclaim Our Health* (2022).

While on the subject of farming, I would like to mention a report published in 2022 by Sustain, the alliance of organisations and communities working together for a better system of food, farming and fishing (https://www.sustainweb.org). The title of the report is *Unpicking food prices: where does your food pound go and why do farmers get so little?*

The report examines in detail where the money spent on five everyday food items – cheese, apples, beefburgers, carrots, and bread – goes, and why that is important to know. It is shocking to read what a small proportion of what we pay for our food products ends up in the farmers' and growers' pockets. After intermediaries and retailers take their cut, farmers and growers are on occasion left with less than 1% of the profit. Meanwhile, we are expecting them to take care of our precious countryside and Nature. They look after 70% of the land in the UK, while trying to make a living, deal with climate change and look after their workforce. Surely, they deserve a lot more than the measly 1% of the profit.

ORGANIC, AGRO-ECOLOGICAL, OR BIODYNAMIC FARMING?

Photo by Oliver Edwards https://oliveredwards.co.uk/

Do you ever wonder what the difference is between organic, agro-ecological and biodynamic farming?

All these three ways of farming have healthy soil in mind, and working with nature, not against it.

For this book I interviewed Guy Singh-Watson - organic farmer, Fred Price – agro-ecological farmer, but I also spoke to a remarkable Dutch couple, Mariel and Gerbrand, who are not farmers, but owners and guardians of the 'Mengelmoestuin', an organic biodynamic garden in Ammerstol, the Netherlands. I learned quite a bit about farming from all three interviews. It is not as easy as many people think, especially if you want to achieve some kind of balance and not submit the environment to your will.

Organic, agro-ecological, and biodynamic farming are quite similar, but there is an area where biodynamics is different: the observation of the Earth's rhythms and the cosmos. For example, the movements of the sun, moon and the planets are studied to decide when the best time is to grow and harvest. The growth of plants is affected by the forces and impulses originating from the different zodiac signs. Whenever the moon goes through a certain zodiac sign there is a positive effect on the plant types that respond to this sign. There are four groups of plants that each respond to three zodiac signs: root plants, leaf plants, blossom plants and fruit plants.

SEASONAL EATING

Seasonal eating – or eating as Nature intended - has never been more topical. As I'm writing this, the UK is trying to cope with a shortage of cucumbers, tomatoes, and other salad ingredients. It is the end of February, and we rely for a large part on import of these vegetables from countries like, Spain and Morocco, or from the greenhouses in the Netherlands. Some of these vegetables are also grown in greenhouses in the UK, but the horrendous energy prices that we have been facing since Russia's invasion of the Ukraine and the cutting down of their natural gas exports to European countries meant that producers cut the number of crops they planted during the winter to cut the costs of heating the greenhouses. The lack of help for UK growers with the high energy prices and the complex supply chains don't help the situation either.

Bad weather in Europe and North Africa slashed the harvests quite dramatically. To give an example of how much we depend on those countries, the UK imports about 25% of its tomatoes from Morocco and about 20% from Spain. The weather in the UK was a problem too, as the cold snap we experienced before Christmas 2022 damaged field crops such as cabbages and carrots.

Of course, I shouldn't forget to mention Brexit here, as bureaucracy, border delays, etc. have an impact on the vegetable shortage too. Brexit has made trading with the UK much more complicated and as a result we are at the bottom of the list for EU exporters.

No matter how you look at the issue, however, climate change is the big factor in all this. We should be more self-sufficient as a country and not rely so much on imported fruit and vegetables.

Instead of supermarkets putting limits on the number of products people are allowed to buy, maybe they should focus on the seasonal vegetables that are not limited and readily available, but I guess most people prefer a salad over a turnip. Consumers want choice all year around and because most fruit and vegetables are always available, no matter what time of the year it is, many of our seasonal vegetables have been demoted and are not that popular. When did you last eat turnips or swede?

In my view it has a lot to do with a lack of cooking skills. I'm sure if you had a nice recipe for the 'unpopular' veg, you would maybe give it a try. How about parmesan-crusted crushed turnips? Or a warming root vegetable gratin?

When thinking about seasonal eating, ask yourself, "What is the earth producing during this season?", and try to go for those products.

The Hungry Gap

While on the subject of seasonal eating, I have to mention the 'Hungry Gap'.

When most of the winter crops have been harvested, but the spring crops are still growing, is when there is a 'Hungry Gap'. Trying to eat seasonally is a bit more challenging during this period. Fortunately, there are still some great vegetables available such as spring greens or purple-sprouting broccoli, if you're not a fan of these there is another solution: frozen or canned vegetables.

Many people think that frozen or canned vegetables (and fruit) are less healthy than fresh produce, but frozen fruit and vegetables are picked at their peak ripeness and are frozen instantly, so they actually contain a lot of nutrients. Most vegetables are blanched before they are frozen to kill bacteria and keep their texture, colour, and flavour. This does lead to a loss of some water-soluble vitamins, but in general there are plenty of nutrients left and the nutrient levels stay fairly stable after freezing.

Canned fruit and vegetables have undergone a little more processing and can lose more nutrients, but overall, they are still relatively healthy. My only worry about canned produce is the lining of the cans. Many cans are lined with plastic (bisphenol A or BPA), a potentially unhealthy chemical that can leak into the food. I personally prefer glass jars.

People who grow their own vegetables will probably have some surplus veggies in their freezers or otherwise preserved. There is nothing more rewarding than eating some of last year's homegrown runner beans during the 'Hungry Gap'.

VITAMIN 'SUNSHINE'

There is a nutrient that has an unusual link with Nature, as not only will you find it in certain foods, the sun plays a big role in its production. It is vitamin D, which, to be precise, is actually a complex hormone rather than a vitamin, although most people are calling it a vitamin. It has many functions in the body, such as regulation of the immune system and bone health.

Unlike other vitamins, vitamin D is made in the skin from exposure to sunlight. The ultraviolet B rays of the sun cause a reaction in the skin that produces previtamin D3. First by the liver, then by the kidneys, this is converted to the active form of vitamin D. It then binds to vitamin D receptors all through the body so it can do its job in different places.

Vitamin D3 can also be found in certain foods such as fatty fish, liver, egg yolk, red meat, cheese, butter, cod liver oil, and fortified foods (foods with added vitamin D).

It is not only vitamin D3 that is found in humans and animals, there is also vitamin D2. Vitamin D2 is formed by UV radiation in certain plants and can be found in mushrooms or sprouted seeds for instance. For us humans, vitamin D3 is better absorbed and used in the body than vitamin D2.

Vitamin D is a fat-soluble vitamin, unlike vitamin C that is water-soluble and is excreted if there is excess. Fat-soluble vitamins need bile acids to be absorbed and any excess will be stored in the body for later use. That is why it is more likely and problematic to overdose on fat-soluble vitamins than water-soluble ones.

Only about 10-20% of our vitamin D3 intake is from foods, the other 80-90% should come from exposure to sunlight. And that is where the problem begins. How often do we have enough sunshine, and can we expose ourselves enough to obtain the required intake of this valuable vitamin?

It is not just a problem in the UK. Almost 50% of the world's population do not get enough vitamin D. Around 1 billion people worldwide are suffering from vitamin D deficiency.

Photo by Canva

There are many factors involved in the low vitamin D status of people:

- *Seasonal lack of sunshine.*
- *Not enough outdoor activities.*
- *Reduced vitamin D production in the skin when people are ageing. When you are older, it takes longer to produce vitamin D.*
- *Limited exposure to the sun (people who are homebound, people whose profession keeps them indoors, religious dress codes, etc.).*
- *Medical conditions that cause fat malabsorption, e.g., Crohn's disease.*
- *Obesity (as vitamin D is fat-soluble so it can build up in fat under the skin and is not then available for use).*
- *Dark skin (more about that later).*
- *Medications that can deplete vitamin D such as Metformin or steroids.*

So, we can produce large amounts of vitamin D ourselves when we strip off and expose lots of skin to the sun. But how long should we be in the sun and when? And isn't too much sun causing skin cancer?

Vitamin D production happens quite quickly. In about half the time it takes for our skin to be sun-burned, we can make a good amount of vitamin D. But we need to expose a bit more than just our face and arms. The more skin we expose, the more vitamin D we can make.

People with a very light skin need only about 15 minutes of decent sun exposure to obtain the vitamin D they need. However, people with a dark skin will need up to 2 hours to produce the same amount of vitamin D.

Why do dark-skinned people need more sun to produce vitamin D? It has to do with melanin, the pigment that gives skin its colour. Melanin protects the skin against damage from too much ultraviolet light and by blocking the rays of the sun, less ultraviolet light enters the skin and as a result, less vitamin D is produced. So, the darker the skin, the longer it takes to produce the necessary vitamin D.

It also depends on where we live. People in the UK make a lot less vitamin D than those living in Africa, near the equator, where the sun is shining all year round. It also depends on what time of day the sun exposure occurs. Between 11am and 3pm the rays of the sun are strongest in the UK because of the angle of the sun. The closer to noon that the skin is exposed to the sun, the better the angle of the sun is, so the more vitamin D is produced. However, there is also a much higher chance of burning the skin and an increased risk of non-melanoma skin cancer if the skin is overexposed to such strong rays.'

To know if the sun is strong, here is a useful tip: look at your shadow and see if it is shorter than your height; if it is, the ultra-violet rays of the sun are strong.

Of course, there is always a risk when exposing the skin to the sun. But there is another risk: overprotection from the sun increases vitamin D deficiency and vitamin D deficiency has been linked to various types of cancer, autoimmune diseases, bone diseases etc. This is quite a dilemma. What to do? Use factor 50 sun cream, stay out of the sun completely?

Cancer Research UK recommends protecting our skin from sunburn between 11am and 3pm by wearing protective clothes, a hat and sunglasses and using sun cream on body parts that cannot be covered. Excessive sun exposure should be avoided and particularly sunburns during childhood.

I would recommend enjoying the sun safely and taking care not to burn, to ensure making the much-needed vitamin D. Also, remember that even when it is cloudy the sun can still burn as 90% of ultra-violet rays can pass through light cloud. Sand and water reflect ultra-violet rays too, so when on the beach burning will be quicker.

BREAST MILK

Research has shown that the environment in which we live, for example how much exposure to greenery we have, has an effect on our health, but did you know that these effects start even as early as being a baby? Essentially it all starts with the mother and her health during pregnancy, the prenatal period, and it continues in a baby's early life.

Finnish scientists Mirkka Lahdenperä and her colleagues researched the effects of the mother's environment on her breast milk composition. They looked at the greenness of the environment, the vegetation cover diversity and its naturalness, and then looked at the breastmilk oligosaccharides, milk sugars that have effects on the baby's immune system and gut microbiome. What Mirrka and her colleagues found, was that those mothers who live in a more varied green environment, had increased and more diverse oligosaccharides in their breastmilk, which would positively influence the baby's health. The research was published in January 2023.

FORAGING

Wild food is becoming more and more popular, and so is foraging.

Every spring there is the wild garlic hype for instance, when you will find more pesto recipes on social media than ever. It is very rewarding though to get into Nature and end up with delicious, fresh food.

Firstly, you really need to know what you are doing, so doing a course or a workshop is a good start. Is it really wild garlic or does it happen to be Lily of the Valley or Lords-and-Ladies? The leaves look very similar, but the leaves of the Lily of the Valley are poisonous, and the Lords-and-Ladies leaves contain sharp oxalate crystals that are a serious irritant. Having a foraging guidebook is extremely helpful.

Secondly, it is important to respect Nature and landowners' properties. Never pick more that you need, don't disturb natural habitats and ask permission if you would like to forage on private land.

Foraging is fun and a great way to (re)connect with Nature. A combination of fresh air, exercise, being close to Nature and ending up with some goodies - what is not to like?

It is also a seasonal activity that will show you different wild foods at different times of the year. Foraging in spring is very different from foraging in autumn when there is a huge selection of mushrooms and fungi to be found.

Nature & Nutrition

My first experience with foraging was when my husband and I booked a foraging course with Wild Food UK in late summer. The walk was led by Fabio, a super-enthusiastic and experienced forager and we were totally blown away by his knowledge and the number of edible plants we found. It was a real eye-opener. I will never forget picking pineapple weed that was growing along a path in the forest and it really smelled like pineapple, or the wood sorrel that tasted like apple peel. Since our first foraging trip we have been foraging for dandelion leaves, cleavers, wood sorrel, blackberries, elderflowers and berries, rosehips, sloe berries and much more. We are hooked.

Our ancestors have always foraged, but not just for food. They would also pick herbs, etc. for their medicinal properties. It is a shame that a lot of ancient knowledge has been lost. It is very rewarding to make your own cough medicine from foraged elderberries or a refreshing peppermint tea to help digestion.

There is one more interesting fact about foraging that I must mention.

Some people make a shopping list before they go shopping, but not only that, the list will be written in the order of the aisles, so they can shop as efficiently as possible, saving time on the distance they have to walk through the supermarket to find products.

There are many animals that do the same thing. For instance, bees use routes that are efficient for foraging nectar. Many young animals learn foraging behaviour from the adults and from each other, by watching other group members forage and by copying their behaviour. Let's hope that many children will learn foraging from their parents and enjoy the process and the harvest.

For this book, I interviewed a forager called Emily, who I had been following on Instagram for quite a while. She finds the most amazing wild plants, herbs, mushrooms, fruits, etc. and uses these wild foods to cook delicious dishes. Read her story in Part Three and be inspired.

FOOD MILES

When you are eating a bar of dark chocolate, do you ever wonder how far this food product has travelled to get from the cocoa farm to your kitchen cupboard? Food miles are the distance the food has travelled from where it was grown/produced to where it is consumed, from 'farm to fork' so to speak, and often the distance that food is travelling has a major impact on our environment, as food products are exported and imported all around the world. Nowadays we can get any food, at any time of the year, and eating seasonally is definitely not as much the standard as it used to be.

However, the biggest environmental impact from food is not from transport, it is from its production. Research showed that, on average, transport emissions account for just 6% of the total carbon footprint of food products.

A good example is the avocado, a very popular food item. If you eat half an avocado 1-2 times a week, on a yearly basis, the greenhouse gas emissions are 15kg, which is the equivalent of driving 39 miles (64km) in your car or heating an average UK house for 2 days. However, growing the avocados uses 3,519 litres of water, which is 54 showers lasting 8 minutes; all these figures are global averages.

Now, let's go back to dark chocolate consumption of 1 bar 1-2 times a week. In one year, your chocolate habit produces 116kg of greenhouse emissions (almost 8x more than the avocado), equivalent to driving your car for 296 miles (476km) or heating the average UK house for 18 days! Annual water use is 1,937 litres.

To give an idea of the scale of food miles, 95% of our fruits and 50% of our vegetables are imported, and in the UK 25% of the miles covered by lorries is food transportation.

So, when we are thinking of the environmental impact of foods, we must remember that the food miles are not the only factor in a food product's total carbon footprint. Vegetables that are grown in a heated greenhouse in the UK can have a higher carbon footprint than those that are imported from abroad and grown in a field for instance. Glass cultivation emits gases (carbon dioxide, methane and nitrous oxide) contributing to global warming, as these gases reduce the amount of heat leaving the earth.

One way of reducing the food miles is to buy seasonal food, grown locally, if you can. Buying directly from the farm has an extra benefit in that there will be less packaging. However, we will also have to bear in mind that if you would drive to the farm by car to pick up your food, this will reduce the environmental benefits.

The carbon footprint is not the only factor to consider, there is also an economic factor at play here. If we would stop importing food, we would take away the livelihood of many communities around the world. Take Africa for instance, where more than 1 million people depend on the UK food trade. 40% of imported fruit and vegetables from Africa arrive here by plane. Air freight normally creates fifty times more carbon emissions than transport by ship, and ten times more than transport by road. However, airfreight accounts for only about 1% of food miles.

With Nature and our planet in mind, environmental choices are important, but they cover much more than just food miles. We could all start with shopping locally, eating seasonally, buying fair-trade products to support third world communities, and if possible, growing our own fruit and vegetables.

PART THREE

CONVERSATIONS ON THE LOST CONNECTION WITH NATURE

*'Those who contemplate the beauty of the earth find reserves
of strength that will endure as long as life lasts.'*

*Rachel Carson
American biologist*

For this book I had twenty-seven conversations with various people on the lost connection with Nature. We talked about their earliest memories of being connected, the effects Nature has on them, why they think modern society has lost its connection with Nature and much more. Everyone was asked the same questions and I also answered the questions myself. The result is twenty-eight very different stories.

I'll light the way.

When did you start to connect with Nature?

Thinking back to my childhood, I have so many memories of being in Nature.

I was very lucky that my parents loved travelling and being outdoors. It is too late to ask them, as unfortunately they are no longer with us, but I would have loved to know if their enthusiasm for the great outdoors came from living in a big city from birth or that it was because of a genuine love of Nature. I guess it must have been a bit of both. My father was quite an impulsive man, so there was always plenty of adventure.

There are some memories that stand out for me, the most important one being my little school allotment that I mentioned before. My own little paradise, where I was growing vegetables and flowers. I can still picture the tall Cosmos plants, growing next to the carrots and potatoes. To me miracles happened on that tiny plot of land. I wish every child could be blessed with such an experience.

Another memory I cherish involves my maternal grandmother Anna, who was partially sighted. Grandma was a volunteer in a magnificent garden for the blind, located in the Zuiderpark; the same park where my school allotment was.

This garden for the blind was centered around smelling, feeling, tasting, and listening.

Fragrant plants and herbs, a water feature, and everything had a sign in braille.

We used to visit my grandma there regularly, as she spent a lot of time in that garden. I loved walking around on my own, pretending to be blind, to feel what the other visitors would experience. A great exercise in mindfulness, and I learned a lot about plants and herbs.

The best memory for me though, taking me back to Nature as a child, were the many camping holidays we spent abroad. We travelled all over Europe and witnessed the most spectacular scenery, Nature at its best. Majestic mountains and crystal-clear lakes in Austria, Switzerland and Italy, wild rivers, and spooky caves in France, and crawling out of the tent every morning, straight into Nature. I am so grateful for these amazing experiences. They did instill a deep connection to Nature and a massive feeling of wonder.

My parents surely introduced us to Nature from an early age. My mother had 'green fingers' and despite the fact we lived in a top-floor flat, there was plenty of greenery indoors, and outdoors on the small balcony. Every opportunity there was to take us outdoors was grabbed with both hands. Visits to parks, boat rides or after-dinner visits to the beach in the summer.

Once my parents had a garden, they started to grow their own vegetables and at some point my father even got an allotment so he would have even more space to grow his own vegetables. Not sure my mother was impressed when he harvested twenty red cabbages in one go….

Did you ever lose the connection and get out of tune with Nature?

While I am writing this, I'm feeling fairly disconnected. Just over two weeks ago, I had foot surgery and was told to rest my leg; no walking, no daily dog walks, no Nature, other than looking out of the window into the garden. It is week three now and not only am I climbing the walls, but I am finding that being cooped up in the house, while outside there is a winter wonderland with snow and ice, is almost unbearable. Yes, it is cold outside, but I would happily go for a walk if I could, to be able to see what Mother Earth has on display for us this winter, and to get some much-needed fresh air.

It definitely has affected my mood, and of course I'm feeling all stiff from just sitting down all day. I am struggling and I am feeling suffocated and drained. My sleep has also been affected by it, as I'm not getting the necessary morning exposure to sunlight.

I can honestly say that the lack of Nature-immersion is overshadowing the pain after the surgery. Hopefully in a couple of weeks' time I will be able to reconnect with Nature properly again.

But to answer the initial question, I lost the connection with Nature a little when I was a teenager. I wanted to fit in and the group I was hanging out with didn't really 'do' Nature. However, I always kept an interest in herbs, astrology, nutrition, and alternative medicine, and I enjoyed being in my parents' garden, so I wasn't totally disconnected.

How did you reconnect?

I started to reconnect properly again when I was a student and was suffering from anxiety and depression. My way out was a cycle ride through the polder, where I felt best: open spaces, exposed to the elements, connected to Nature.

In the meantime, my parents had embarked on a new adventure and had bought a derelict farmhouse in France. This turned out to be my retreat, my place of healing, and I spent a lot of time there, deeply connected to the unspoiled countryside. I still remember lying in bed, listening to the owls and cuckoos, feeling totally calm and content.

For me, becoming a naturopathic nutritional therapist was a logical step in finding my calling and doing what is closest to my heart. It took a while….

After getting a Bachelor of Education degree and working as a teacher and trainer, I then got a Bachelor of Arts degree in Human Resource Management and I worked as an HR Manager for various companies, until I started travelling. What was supposed to be a year out, turned into the biggest adventure. I met my husband, a fellow traveller from the UK, during my travels in 1992 and he is still my favourite travel companion.

We lived and worked in Hong Kong, Vietnam, and Saudi Arabia, until we came to the UK in 1999. During our time abroad I never felt disconnected from Nature as we always managed to find natural beauty where we lived and on our travels through the regions.

What effects does the connection with Nature have on your life?

To me Nature is my healer, my go-to when I'm feeling down and my charging station when I'm tired. Nature makes me feel alive.

Photo by Kerry J https://kerryjphotography.co.uk/

Nature is also my inspiration. Being an amateur painter, I paint a lot of landscapes and I try to capture the natural beauty as best as I can. I am forever taking pictures when I am out and about, collecting reference material for future art projects.

This year, more than any year before, I have experienced the healing powers of Nature.

At the beginning of this year my darling dad passed away and this hit me harder than I expected. We knew for a long time that his time with us was almost up, but as with any loss of a beloved relative, it was still very unexpected and sudden. During the Covid pandemic we had become much closer, even though we were in different countries. We FaceTimed each other every other day. Dealing with my grief has been made easier because of the time we were able to spend in Nature. Long, quiet walks in Cornwall and Yorkshire have given me the peace and quiet to reflect on the impact my dad has had on my life and the gratitude for having had him as a father. His passing was part of the cycle of life, part of Nature, and it is OK. Nature is unquestionably a healer.

One of the most beautiful quotes I have read while researching for this book, is one from Jon Young, a wilderness-tracking teacher. It is mentioned in Richard Louv's book, *The Nature Principle*. To me it sums up the connection with Nature beautifully:

> *"I think of the Nature connection as more nutritive, in an emotional, intellectual, spiritual sense. It's such a profoundly deep part of who we are as human beings, and our potential."*

Why do you think modern society has lost its connection with Nature?

Working as a naturopathic nutritional therapist, I am often seeing clients in my practice, who are quite disconnected from Nature, being stuck in a vicious cycle of stress and overwork, leading to physical and mental health problems, that in turn are aggravating the stress even more. Asking a simple question like "how often do you exercise outdoors?" frequently gets a negative answer, explained by a lack of time, and the honestly admitted gravitational pull from phones and other devices.

Social media is having a hold on people, and it often becomes an addiction. It is time-consuming and, in many cases, it gives a false picture of the world we live in, while in reality there is a world out there, that is driven by productivity, competition and consumerism, with real people, with real issues, who are desperately trying to keep up.

Don't get me wrong, I use social media too for my business and to keep in touch with far-away friends, and I do see the benefits. Some of the wonderful people, who have contributed to this book, I would never have met if it wasn't for social media!

I personally think that the real connection with Nature comes from the connection with the seasons. There is nothing better than noticing the subtle changes in our environment and altering the way we live in response. Living according to the seasons gives me a sense of purpose. I always say, "I wish I was a bear, so I could go into hibernation in winter". Winter is not my most sociable time....

Living according to the seasons also means eating according to the seasons.

There is often little knowledge of seasonal foods, the benefits of adding herbs and spices to the diet or, in a wider context, where food comes from. Strawberries really do not grow naturally in the UK in winter….

Of course, I am not blaming anyone for this lack of knowledge. I was lucky enough to grow up in a food-orientated household, where everything was cooked from scratch, and fruit and vegetables were seasonal. Obviously, some people are more interested in food than others. I have seen clients who could not cook a proper meal from scratch, as they were never taught how to do this. For those clients, mealtimes were always quite stressful, and they would reach for processed, convenience foods, that were far from 'natural'. I will go into the link between Nature and nutrition later, because to me it is fundamental for our very existence and the future of our planet.

In your opinion, what is the best way for people to get in tune with Nature?

To me the best way to get in tune with Nature is to learn to use all your senses when out and about, and to pay attention. To be able to smell the seasons, to hear the birds, to see the insects, to feel the weather. For example, don't use your mobile phone when walking the dog. Apart from being able to be more engaged with your pet, it will also show you the beauty of Nature and will make you more aware of what is going on around you.

I really want to mention 'mindfulness' here. Mindfulness is basically thinking of what you're thinking, being aware of your surroundings and choosing to focus your attention on something in a positive and helpful way. For example, when you're walking through a forest and you focus on each step you make, feeling the soil under your feet, you're already being mindful.

Another way to get in tune with Nature is living seasonably, developing a relationship with the seasons. Following the seasons, noticing the seasonal signs and changes, eating seasonal foods.

In practical terms I would say, "grow something", herbs or an indoor plant if you don't have any outdoor space. Organise an outdoor activity with friends or family and reflect on how you feel when you come home.

Cook a meal from scratch with seasonal produce and recognise how those seasonal vegetables taste just right for the time of the year. And whatever you're eating, ask yourself where this food is coming from and what was involved to get it on your plate. The shorter the distance from grower to plate, the more you will experience a connection with Nature.

And last, but not least, enjoy the conversations in this book, and be open to the advice that is given.

🌿 Meet Abby – Green Hub Volunteer and A-level student

Abby Pearce is currently a student at 6th form college, studying psychology, graphic design, and film studies. She joined the Green Hub Project for Teens in July 2021 to learn more about the benefits of Nature and gardening on the mind, and to support her own wellbeing. After volunteering there for a few months, she understood the positive change these sessions in the garden made on her mental health, and became a mentor, and subsequently a senior volunteer, to help new teens discover how the garden can help them.

She loves photography and the ability to capture life, as well as zoom in on the things that people often overlook. Nature photography in particular helps her freeze things that are constantly changing, making it possible to look back and witness growth. With a huge interest in the human mind and behaviour, Abby is going on to study psychology at degree level, progressing towards a career in psychological research.

Abby's story is about her newfound connection with the natural world through The Green Hub Project, as well as focusing on the adolescent perspective and benefits of Nature.

When did you start to connect with Nature?

I started to connect with Nature during my early childhood, National Trust walks were essentially my life back then. I'd go all the time with my mum and family friends, as all us kids were the same age from the same village, so the majority of my childhood was just being in Nature. The freedom was just amazing. Running through a field as a child is just the most brilliant feeling, and I suppose it still is, but I think we forget to do things like that when we grow up. And although I have great memories of those moments, I didn't really appreciate back then how truly amazing it was.

I've participated in the Green Hub Project for Teens as a volunteer since July 2021, and it's made me appreciate Nature so much more. I got to understand how healthy Nature is for the soul and mind, and it was probably here that I properly connected with Nature on a deeper level for the first time.

Did you ever lose the connection and get out of tune with Nature?

As I got older, the possibilities of fun and games broadened so much. When I was given an iPad, my entire idea of fun changed. It was all very new, different, and high tech, and I thought it was easier to get out an iPad and get as much or even more enjoyment as getting ready, driving somewhere, and going on a walk. I guess I just forgot what it was like to be out in Nature, because you kind of lose yourself in modern technology. You forget how important Nature is for yourself. There's also a notion that because everyone else is doing it, you don't want to be the one left out; an iPad was cooler than going for a walk with your parents.

How did you reconnect?

I'm not a super sociable person, but I love socialising, and need it, but it takes away a lot of my energy and I need alone time. I absolutely love walking; it is so peaceful. I often walk with my friends and their dogs, but sometimes I just go out on my own, having that space to think and breathe. When you're surrounded by the beauty of the Nature, there are no distractions, like you forget the stress of life for a little while. I also think that you notice things more if you actually just take a minute to look around whilst being on a walk. There is so much beauty in Nature and it is wonderful to be part of it and simply exist in it.

I am very lucky in that I have more like-minded friends, who understand the world how I see it: calm. They're not heavy partygoers or people who stay up very late. We all have similar hobbies like art, reading and writing. Very peaceful hobbies, that allow people to stop and slow down, whereas social media and everything else in the world moves so fast.

If you're an extroverted person, I think it's much harder to be able to slow down and see Nature for what it is.

What effects does the connection with Nature have on your life?

Nature has made a huge impact on my life. I was seeing a chiropractor for scoliosis during my GCSE exams, and I never realised how much it was going to affect, not only my physical health, but my mental health. I was in a lot of pain most of the time, and it really started to get to me that I was incapable of doing so many things suddenly, and at such an important time. I was frustrated, but also really upset. I had no one to blame so I just had to deal with it. During one of our sessions, my chiropractor mentioned the Green Hub Project for Teens.

Essentially you get to do gardening in this wonderful little garden, as well as crafting activities with other teenagers and some adult volunteers. I thought, "Why not give it a try?" I also struggle with confidence, and I was about to go to college, so I thought this might help me. I gave it a go, and I loved it.

Although I love the crafting activities, the most exciting part of Green Hub was when I planted my first tomato seeds. They were so important to me and every week I remember watering them and checking they were all right, looking after them until the fruits were ripe. It's just the most amazing feeling because you know that you made that happen. The progression of growth is just amazing.

As I have been part of the Green Hub Project for quite a while now, I have become a senior volunteer, meaning I am still being able to attend the sessions and see the progression of the garden. It means that I can help others now to understand the connection with Nature as well.

It is so good to see all these new people coming in, knowing that we're giving them a space to slow down. You don't have to do gardening; you can just sit in the garden and enjoy being in that setting. I remember how immediately calming and comforting it was for me, even at my first session. You start to realise how much taking a pause from life calms down your mind. Slowing down can help you figure out your thoughts, but you can also just forget about them for a minute. It's like stopping life for a little bit and just existing in the moment. And I think that that is helpful in general for mental health. It calms you and makes you feel better about yourself and life.

You don't have to be a more introverted, quieter person to be able to experience everything that you can in the garden. I think anyone who is willing to try can join in and find peace, although it might take longer for some people. Soil is healing and your hands being in soil is really good for you. We were put on this planet and Nature was there first. And we're here to enjoy it and I think everyone is capable of that.

Why do you think modern society has lost its connection with Nature?

I think it has a lot to do with evolving technology and this massive digital era. Everything is so focused on people, the appearance, the relationship status, or how successful they are.

I know that things like media and gaming is connecting people and bringing them together, which is great. Obviously, there are a lot of disadvantages of social media as well, given the content available for anyone to access, and the thin line between truth and lies. Technology is constantly growing and getting more advanced, the progression of the world is happening very fast. Most people have forgotten how to stop, slow down, and just be, because everything's changing all the time and moving too quickly.

In your opinion, what is the best way for people to get in tune with Nature?

Find some space to be alone outside. For people suffering from any mental health condition, like anxiety or depression, the worst thing you can do is sit in a dark room.

I think a lot of parents don't really understand that people with anxiety and depression need some space to be alone. Obviously talking helps but walking on your own is so calming and it gives you time to actually think about everything in your head, rather than just let it be there and make you more nervous or upset. And breathe in the fresh air, it is refreshing, and it can give you this new, different way of seeing things, like your mind sort of opens up.

Maybe things aren't so bad after all. I know that being outside in Nature is not necessarily going to cure everything for all, but for me it definitely helped, and I think it could be the same for a lot of people I know who are of my age.

Something I really enjoy is taking photos of Nature. It is nice to capture moments in Nature, especially the change, because everything is changing in the garden constantly and you can't really take the same photo twice. I'm quite a creative person, I like capturing things. I started to take photos of what is going on in the garden. Capturing it for people who maybe don't really look at Nature. It's almost like it's always there, watching and waiting for you to really see it.

🌿 Meet Amir – Physics professor-turned-farmer in Iran

Amir Esmaeil Mosaffa is the son of two professors of Persian literature in Teheran.

Until 9 years ago he was a professor of physics at the Sharif University of Teheran, Iran; then he discovered the joy of farming.

This move from the very abstract world of string theory and 11-dimensional supergravity to growing walnuts and pomegranates, and growing grafted walnut saplings, piqued my curiosity, so I was very grateful when an Iranian friend of mine introduced me to Amir and we were able to talk on Skype.

Living in Teheran with his wife, a GP and nutritionist, Amir regularly travels to his farms that are in three different locations, the walnut orchard being the furthest away, about 250km from Teheran, so he spends a lot of time on the road.

When did you start to connect with nature?

I wasn't connected with Nature when I was a child, I never had an interest in plants or trees. I was exposed to Nature, but I did not have a passion for it, apart from animals.

The most original love I have is for animals. I can say that I prefer almost all animals to all humans.

My connection with Nature didn't start until 10 years ago, when I discovered the miracle that are walnut trees.

I studied physics at university, got a PhD, and just loved science. I was far away from anything 'real'. There came a moment, several years ago, when I wasn't happy with my work environment anymore. Given the situation in Iran, you become, directly or indirectly, a political person. When I started lecturing, as well as doing research, I got deeply involved in politics and came under a lot of pressure. The farming didn't happen as a result of this, but it just coincided with what was happening in my professional life at the time.

I'm a huge fan of walnuts. Since I was a child, I have loved eating them, but I also love the shape of the trees. The fact that those trees can live for hundreds of years always fascinated me. I had an epiphany when I was thinking about the trees continuously bearing fruits every year and realised what a miracle it is. I don't get overwhelmed easily, but that was definitely one of those moments. I realised I didn't just want to eat the nuts, I wanted to work with these trees.

I started reading about walnut trees and being a researcher, I got totally hooked on all the information I found. This is how I found out about the concept of grafting and budding, to improve trees. I started to self-educate myself with YouTube videos, etc. and within a very short time I became a very accomplished walnut tree-grafter. I was still doing my physics job and had no intention of leaving it. In the meantime, I met someone who had a PhD in walnut tree management (yes, there really is such a thing) and we worked together on some innovations and wrote a paper on it. It was never published as we were both too lazy, but it did set a standard on how walnut trees are grafted in Iran nowadays. And this was the start of it all.

Having a scientific and research background and an analytical mind have been useful in my connection with Nature. I see the miracle of Nature as processes, systems, that are happening; I don't just see the beauty, unlike artists for instance. I research and study, for example, how to make compost.

Alongside the walnuts, there was still my academic life, and I was gradually getting fed up with it. For the first time in my life, I was doing something and seeing the results, not in years or months, but in weeks or even days; it was fascinating. It was all so far removed from 11-dimensional space time, etc. I still love physics though, but I found a new love, a passion. I did resign as a professor, but I wasn't really a farmer yet. That came later.

Depending on the time of the year, I spend time at the farms. I have a farm where I grow pomegranates, about 100km east of Teheran, a smaller farm with an orchard of about 300 walnut trees, and a nursery that produces grafted walnut tree saplings, 55km southwest of Teheran. This year we'll produce around 60,000 saplings.

Did you ever lose the connection and got out of tune with nature?

Since I got in touch through the farming, I haven't lost the connection with Nature.

What effects does the connection with nature have on your life?

I found a new love in Nature, and I was ready for it, and it has made me a very happy person. It is my fuel for life and life is full of surprises as every farm is different. Nature is very resilient, and you have to work with it.

I'm a happier, more harmonious and forgiving person, and I feel healthier.

Why do you think modern society has lost its connection with nature?

In modern society there is a lot of pressure of trends, fashion, and the modern way of living.

Now I have nothing against modernity, but the point is that a lot of people do things unnecessarily, without understanding why they are doing it. Many people do things because they were told to do so, like youngsters going into higher education without asking themselves if that is what they really want to do. They just do it because they were told to. Children are being sent to a ridiculous amount of after school activities because the parents think that is useful, without asking the children what it is what they really want.

People have lost their authenticity. The authenticity and originality of one's desires and interests has become lost. This is a big problem in my country, people are not original. When you are original, you know what you desire, what drives you.

It is the same with where people live, what scenery they choose to see every day, what food to eat, etc.

Modern people have become control freaks and Nature is all about patience, and this is not a good combination.

The mobile phones are partially to blame too. I never had a mobile phone until I started to go to the farms and my wife insisted on me getting one so we could stay in touch. I don't have a smart phone, I have a 'dumb' phone and even that I dislike. Why would you buy a phone with lots of buttons? The more buttons your phone has, the more anxiety you get. Why do you need so many options on a car? It's all because it is a trend. People are not original; they don't really have the time and the convenience to think what they really want or need. People are distracted and they don't even know it.

In your opinion, what is the best way for people to get in tune with nature?

Get exposed to Nature. It is as simple as that.

I invite my friends who have children to come to the farm and the children can plant a tree. That is their tree then and every year the harvest from that tree is theirs. Or I invite friends to come and help me with the grafting, when I think they need to get out. I don't really need help, but it is a good way to get them exposed to Nature. I helped a couple to find a piece of land and they have turned it into a beautiful garden in a couple of years. These are some examples of exposure, but there are so many options. Just go out and find Nature.

Follow good examples. I don't use pesticides on the farm and over time other people in the village also started to ban pesticides.

❧ Meet Andrew – Beekeeper and Retired RHS Principal Entomologist

Andrew Halstead is originally from North Hertfordshire, but is now based in Woking, Surrey.

After a career of more than 41 years as an entomologist at the Royal Horticultural Society Garden Wisley, Andrew remains a very busy man. As well as being a keen beekeeper, he holds a wide range of positions, all linked to Nature in one way or another:

Fellow of the Royal Entomological Society, Past President of the British Entomological and Natural History Society and currently a Council member, Member of Amateur Entomologists Society, Dipterists Forum, Bees, Wasps and Ants Recording Society and Surrey Wildlife Trust.

He is also Chairman of the Weybridge Division of Surrey Beekeepers Association, Chairman of the Goldsworth Park Allotments Society, and a Trustee of Horsell Common Preservation Society.

I got to know Andrew through my husband, who is also a member of the Weybridge Beekeepers. Together with a few other members they are setting up a teaching apiary, where people wanting to become beekeepers can gain some practical experience after they have attended the theory course.

Whenever we see an unidentified insect or plant, we always ask Andrew as he has immense knowledge of the natural world.

When did you start to connect with Nature?

I think my interest in Nature was always there. As a child I used to collect caterpillars to see what sort of moth they would turn into. I was brought up in a semi-rural part of North Hertfordshire, at a time when children were allowed to go off on their own to explore the countryside.

My parents were into gardening. They were of the war generation, so growing your own food was quite important. My father kept bees, but again, that probably was because of the wartime, to have a source of sweetener, as sugar was strictly rationed but obtainable for beekeepers. After the war he kept his bees, and it was a lifelong interest for him.

My parents didn't have much spare time to be outdoors with me; my father had an ironmongers' shop and my mother, who originally trained as a teacher, became a housewife and then helped in the shop.

Did you ever lose the connection and get out of tune with Nature?

No, luckily, I still have a connection with Nature. Even as a teenager I stayed in tune with it, as I was quite a loner and enjoyed being outdoors.

Going through school, doing A-levels, I chose the subjects that I thought were the simplest options, the things that appealed to me and I found easier. So, I chose to do zoology, botany, and chemistry.

I had no idea what to study at university, but the careers adviser suggested agriculture.

I studied agricultural sciences at Nottingham University. After the first year, we had to specialise, and I started to head towards entomology and soil biology. Getting a job after university was difficult and I decided to do an MSc in Crop Protection at Bangor University. In the 1970s, if you wanted employment in entomology, the best options were working in the field of killing insects.

After my MSc I got a job with the Royal Horticultural Society as an assistant to the senior entomologist and I stayed there for over 41 years, retiring after several years as the principal entomologist.

What effects does the connection with Nature have on your life?

Being connected with the natural world has given me a lifelong interest in ecology and conservation, and it has provided me with the career working as the Royal Horticultural Society's Entomologist.

However, as a child, not having much experience of the world, I just took Nature for granted.

For example, given my father was a beekeeper, I grew up with bees from an early age and was always helping out. When my father died, I took over his bees and brought them to Surrey, but I do not have an emotional connection with them, even though I am a keen beekeeper.

It is not until you are an adult that you notice how things have changed and are continuing to change. You are aware that there is not as much wildlife and wild countryside as there used to be, farming practices have changed quite considerably and so on. Climate change is having a noticeable impact on insect distribution. Some southern England species are spreading further north, while other species that require cooler conditions are losing ground. There is a feeling of regret, for instance when a place of natural beauty has become a housing estate. There is a sense of loss.

Why do you think modern society has lost its connection with Nature?

I think modern society has lost its connection with Nature because the times have changed.

When I was younger, information about plants and wildlife came from books and there was often a local natural history society you could join. Nowadays, the internet is the major supplier of information. You can be in the middle of nowhere, take a picture of a plant or animal on your mobile phone, post it on an appropriate Facebook group, and within a few minutes someone will have identified it for you. You can record a bird song, go to an appropriate app and the unseen bird will be identified. Technology is wonderful, but the people involved never meet each other in person. The surviving local natural history societies are struggling to attract new young members, which does not bode well for their future. When information about wildlife is available at the click of a button, is that knowledge likely to be retained? I suspect it is not.

These days there are some superb wildlife films shown on TV that reach a wide audience. These films ought to stimulate interest in the natural world, but it may be that they make Britain's wildlife seem a bit dull and tame by comparison.

*In your opinion, what is the best way for
people to get in tune with Nature?*

To get in tune with Nature, start at a young age and hope that the young people stay interested in the natural world around them. Most people will prefer a particular aspect of natural history, whether it be plants, fungi, birds, mammals, insects, etc. By focusing on a particular topic, expertise in identifying species and learning about their biology can be more readily gained than by a scatter gun approach to the whole area of natural history.

There are plans for a GCSE qualification in natural history, which may help with this process.

The new Natural History GCSE will allow young people to explore the world by learning about organisms and environments, environmental and sustainability issues, and get a deeper knowledge of the natural world in which we all live. They will also develop the skills to help them carve a future career in the natural world if they wish to – for example observation, description, recording and analysis, through sustained and structured field studies.

At a simpler level, just put away the phone/computer and go for a walk in the nearby woods, a park, a Nature reserve, etc. and use your eyes to see the variety of plants, birds, insects, and other creatures that are out there. Take the time to stop and stare, instead of marching directly from A to B.

ॐ Meet Charlie – Yoga teacher and Designer

Charlie Leigh was brought up in Yorkshire & the Lake District. When she was 19 years old, she left the Lakes to go travelling and enjoyed two snowboarding seasons in British Columbia, Canada. After her travels she studied Textiles, Fashion & Fibre at Winchester School of Art, specialising in Men's knitwear design. Charlie based her collections on natural phenomena such as murmurations and the Northern lights. She loves craft and texture, as well as natural fibres.

After university Charlie explored further afield and lived in Australia & New Zealand, where she enjoyed many adventures, as well as completing internships at fashion houses in Sydney. When Charlie returned to the UK, she settled in Guildford where she entered her career in advertising & marketing, utilising her design experience.

Having always enjoyed yoga since she was a student and having practiced different styles across the world, it wasn't until years later that Charlie became a teacher in one of her personal favourite styles – Kundalini Yoga. Following this came yin & restorative yoga, as well as gong healing and reiki.

Charlie is very interested in the deeper practices of yoga, where the focus is on the body's energy channels and connecting mind, body and soul in an intuitive, peaceful way. She incorporates natural energies into all of her classes, as believes the two are closely connected. This includes the moon, crystals, and essential oils to name a few.

I first met Charlie when I attended one of her yoga classes. The Nature Workshops followed, and I have been a fan ever since. The way she integrates Nature into her classes and her grounded personality were the determining factors for asking her to participate in this book.

When did you start to connect with Nature?

Nature was always a large part of my life when I was young. I am from Northern England and growing up I lived in the Yorkshire Dales and the

Lake District. It was not uncommon as a family, to go on a hike, swim in the lakes, dance in streams and run through the heather. As one of four girls, we were always told to go play outside at home too. We didn't have access to mobile phones and tablets in those days.

Looking back, I think it was the areas I lived in and my grandmother, who instilled a true love of Nature in me. We first lived in Yorkshire, in a place called Kirkbymoorside, in a house with a great big garden and a greenhouse. It was gorgeous. My parents weren't keen gardeners.

We didn't have a TV when I grew up, until we moved down south, and my older sister Philippa and I were generally playing outdoors most of the time.

My nan was a keen gardener, and we spent a lot of time with her during the summer holidays. I particularly loved my nan's house, where I would forage, make mud pies and be very content spending the whole day in the trees. I became very close to my nan and her passion for Nature.

Thinking about my late mother reminded me of a ritual. As soon as we were 8 years old, my mother would take us to a particular stream in the Yorkshire Dales, where we had to wash our face and hold out hands in the water. My mother was quite quirky and had crystals and Buddha statues around the house. I guess she did instil some kind of love of Nature in me, without me realising it. When I was about 10 years old, we moved to the Lake District, because it reminded my mother of her own childhood and she wanted to pass it on to us.

But I also think she wanted to go back to heal to be honest.

Did you ever lose the connection and get out of tune with Nature?

Before we moved to the Lake District we also lived in Suffolk, I felt different there as we were sucked in by the digital world and we had a TV. Where you live as a child affects you. It is where the connection comes from.

I also did lose the connection with Nature during a period of trauma in my life. The trauma began when I was around eleven years old and lasted until I was about 28 years old.

From the age of eleven till sixteen years old, I had a very bad home life.

At the time, my mother suffered from depression which turned into alcoholism, and subsequently my father turned to alcohol too. When I was at the age of sixteen my father left us, my mother was unable to look after me, and I left home. I lived with two sisters for a while and then my friend's parents took me in. I was happier there, experiencing a stable home, and I continued college.

After college, rather than going straight to university, I travelled to Canada to spend a couple of seasons snowboarding. Whilst in Canada, I did reconnect with Nature, surrounded by snow, beautiful lakes, and trees. Here, I also tried some plant medicines for the first time and had amazing experiences. I was very happy there, but I came back to the UK when I was twenty-one years old, and it wasn't long until my mother passed away. Two weeks after that happened, I started university, where I didn't know anyone.

A few years later, I also lost my stepfather to suicide. He was lonely after my mum had passed and he was suffering from MS. During this phase in my life, I was at the lowest point to date, and I really disconnected, not only from my environment, but also from my own body. Because of the high stress levels, it was hard to slow down and see the beauty within Nature.

How did you reconnect?

I reconnected with Nature through yoga and love.

My yoga practice started in Canada while travelling. I practiced many different styles when I was travelling through New Zealand and Australia, but after my stepfather's suicide I stopped completely for a couple of years.

At the same time, I was in an unhealthy relationship, where I felt unloved and suppressed. It was only when this relationship ended and I met my current partner Kul, that I restarted my yoga practice in a much deeper way. Kul held the space for me to explore myself and gave me a lot of love and nurturing. As soon as my yoga practice deepened, my connection with Nature blossomed again.

Yoga has been part of my healing, it slowed me down, gave me the ability to connect deeper within myself and allowed me to connect deeper with Nature. When you go 'within' it is easier to stop and notice Nature. Your senses are heightened, and you see things differently. You come to a point where you realise 'we are all one'.

What effects does the connection with Nature have on your life?

Nature brings me deeper into my soul. I always have it around me. In front of my computer, on my desk, I have foraged items like pinecones, feathers, and dried flowers that I can see and feel.

I always have fresh flowers at home and, every day I go for a walk, usually barefoot, to ground and reenergise myself. I find peace and healing through all of this.

The combination of my yoga practice and the plant medicines I also take has made me the person I am today. I have healed so much of my trauma, and I have been able to open my heart and be free again. This led me to teaching these modalities to others. Nature plays a huge role in my everyday life, and I truly believe it connects us to our soul.

Why do you think modern society has lost its connection with Nature?

Everyone has some sort of trauma and I know a lot of people go through similar experiences to those I had. When you feel low and depressed, you often turn to unhealthy foods, the wrong people, and addictions to suppress those feelings. In a state like this, you are often dissociated from your body, and you will find it very hard to do anything for yourself, let alone have the ability or desire to connect to Nature.

I also believe that the amount of technology we use, and I'm even thinking about just walking around while on the phone, hugely interferes with the connection to our surroundings. I am planning a retreat next year in the woods which will be all eco-friendly, connecting with Nature and disconnecting from technology.

In your opinion, what is the best way for people to get in tune with Nature?

Simply starting with a short walk every day, even if it is just pottering around your own garden. Don't take a phone and look at everything around you and look up at the sky. When in woodlands close your eyes and breath in all the beautiful smells from the trees.

If unable to go for a walk, bring Nature into the home with plants that you can take care of and observe.

With my Nature workshops I want to open the door to making Nature part of your life; I want to take people back to the simplicities of life. Creating Nature mandalas, using essential oils, etc. are a beautiful way to make Nature part of your life.

To connect more with Nature you don't need a deep spiritual practice.

🌿 Meet Daniel – Nutritionist, Functional Medicine Practitioner & Author

Daniel O'Shaughnessy is an award-winning nutritionist, certified Functional Medicine Practitioner (IFMCP) and the author of the book, 'Naked Nutrition', an LGBTQ+ Guide to Diet & Lifestyle. He has over 10 years of clinical experience. Daniel studied Nutrition at the Institute of Optimum Nutrition and he is currently doing a Masters in Transdisciplinary Practice at Middlesex University London, focusing on psychedelics.

The reason why I asked Daniel to participate in this book is not just because of his profession, but more because of his extraordinary personal journey.

When did you start to connect with Nature?

I think when I was a child I took Nature for granted, I just wanted to be in the city, even though we lived in a house with a stream, a river, and a field with horses. I was privileged in a way, without realising it, and I didn't think much of it. I didn't realise the cathartic effects of Nature; I didn't have much awareness of what it was doing for me. When I was a kid, I was just living in the moment, rather than analysing, thinking, and checking whether it was good for me or not.

Like many other kids, I loved video games, and being given the choice as a child to go for a walk or sit in front of Nintendo wasn't a hard one. However, I used to love my school cross-country events, and the idea of feeling lost in the never-ending woods was quite a thrill for me in a way. At the time I wasn't aware that trees are a living system, I just thought they were trees.

I don't have any distinct memories of being in Nature as a kid. The only thing I do remember is the field with the horses. On reflection, being with the horses in this field was very healing for me, but at the time I didn't realise that it was having such a positive effect on me. I had an unhappy childhood, and because I didn't have many friends, I would just be with the horses in the paddock all the time; it was my separation from the stress, my escape all the time, it was my separation from the stress, my escape. It was like my body knew it was a good way to find comfort. I found myself more connecting with animals than humans, especially being gay and not realising it properly yet. I loved being on my own and being quiet. My real awareness of what Nature was doing to me came much later in life.

I became more involved with Nature since I started using psychedelics. They make me want to be more in Nature and move away from the city. Since I got my dog, I'm more in Nature to walk her obviously, and if you then add the experience of psychedelics to it, it has just changed my perception of Nature; it also changed the way I think.

Near where I live in London is a little park that is full of these 400-year-old trees, probably even a lot older, but they're the most amazing trees to look at. And whether I'm on a psychedelic or in the aftermath of it, I now appreciate Nature much more and I can really see. I think when you are taking a psychedelic you become more aware and you're more in the moment, but also, everything looks different and more alive.

One of my favorite experiences was at a friend's house last summer, when we were in his garden and did mushrooms. It was the most significant, grounding experience, because I felt like I was connected to the earth, and it just felt like I was wrapped in Nature's protection or love. It was much more of a healing environment than if I would take psychedelics on a retreat, at home or in a building.

Before, I would wake up and would be already thinking about next week, now, with the cumulative effect of psychedelics, I'm living more in the moment and appreciating my surroundings more. I think, as a result, I'm less anxious and I'm also taking in my environment.

When I go for a walk, I'm looking around rather than looking at my phone, or worrying about something, or being anxious. I think the feeling I get from Nature contributes to healing and living.

During lockdown I was always walking around Central London because I love the empty city, but now I would rather go for a walk where I'm going to be in a park.

The other day I was looking at holidays, where before I would probably go for a beach in Spain, now I just want to be alone in a log cabin in the woods. And that is how my mind has changed now, because I know the healing effects of Nature, and I know what it will be like to be in that environment. Maybe it's a sign of getting older and letting go of the party lifestyle, but I don't like anything that is artificial.

*Did you ever lose the connection and
get out of tune with Nature?*

I guess I lost the connection with Nature when I was younger and moved to the big city.

I didn't go out in Nature much, then I became a corporate 9-5 slave and lived for the weekend, drinking, drugs, etc. But also, part of it all was the trauma I had suffered in my life and my lack of self-love that was holding me back.

Looking back, I understand why I didn't love myself, but I'm still wondering why I didn't like myself, why I didn't stand up for myself, why I didn't look after myself.

As mentioned before, I had an unhappy childhood, had trauma at school, where I was bullied severely for being gay and being ginger, so I was always in a stress-induced nightmare. And then obviously, I had to deal with my own sexuality. On top of that, I had some failed relationships, but these weren't huge trigger points.

There are quite a lot of layers of trauma. I kept on asking myself why I didn't stand up for myself more and that was very much a big lesson that I only learned very recently and probably with the help of psychedelics.

The Japanese have this saying that we all have three masks or faces: we have a face that you show the world, a face that you show your friends and family, and a face that you never show anyone. We present ourselves differently to different audiences. So, the level of authenticity is what I was failing at, just putting on this fake mask for everyone, failing myself, and now I just put this authentic mask on and I seem to trigger something by being authentic, as some people think I'm a different person. Since I have connected with Nature, I have met more authentic people. Again, the Japanese come to mind, they have this metaphor Kintsugi, when a pot breaks they put it together with gold, so rather than owning my trauma and becoming my trauma, I don't hide the cracks and imperfections.

How did you reconnect?

One day, a friend suggested I try LSD and I was petrified. I said no because I thought I would lose control. And then I looked at myself and I thought maybe that is the problem. So, he gave me my first LSD tablet and it just ignited the healing; in the space of three hours, I experienced more healing than in the four years of therapy I had before, it was reframing the way I think.

Psychedelics aren't necessarily a miracle cure, yes, they are a miracle, but they're not going to give you any answers. They make the obvious appear in front of your ego, because the ego is where the problem lies. The ego you have is so trained to know the thought patterns you're used to, that if anything comes to confront that, it will protect itself, so there's the effort, there's the best control mechanism so I knew my ways of working and my ways of knowing. And I was in this happy defence system where all the bad stuff that has happened to me in life, I was managing, but to a point where I was still using numbing behaviours like party drugs at the weekend. I got to the point where I knew that I needed to change and that was my epiphany, when I actually had that healing.

Since my childhood trauma I've never been able to cry because I was always told you can't cry. Boys don't cry. I remember that 'Aha' moment, when I woke up from a trip and tears were streaming down my face. I had obviously gone on this journey, and I just remembered these visuals; it was the most healing experience, and it gave me the thirst to work out how this all works, because it changed the way I think. So, I started experimenting with mushrooms and then I had the chance to do ayahuasca, which is Nature in itself. It is a hallucinogenic drink made from the leaves and bark of South American plants. The leaves contain N, N-Dimethyltryptamine (DMT), the psychedelic ingredient, and the bark stops the DMT breaking down in the body. Amazon tribes brew the leaves and bark in a pot for hours and hours, and they add shamanic prayers and energy to it. When you are taking this drink, you are drinking Nature. It is also called 'Mother Earth', or 'Father of the Sky' and it was probably one of the most compelling experiences of Nature I ever had, Nature's medicine.

For me it was something completely new and life changing, it changed the way I went from being suicidal to 'I don't want to kill myself', I completely love myself. I appreciate psychedelics are illegal, but I take them in safe places, and I do ayahuasca in legal settings, like in Portugal, Spain, Mexico, where it is legal. Of course, I can't give people psychedelics, I wouldn't do that, but I can teach them the lessons that I have learned from psychedelics: control, rejection, forgiveness, self-love, etc. and that psychedelics make you feel you can connect with Nature in a deeper way.

From a professional point of view, I was getting fed up with the way we look at nutrition in terms of clients coming to see a practitioner, being fixated on, for example, their cholesterol or their digestive issue but forgetting that underneath the iceberg of all their trauma are their personality traits or their degree of stress. This model isn't working for me and how I operate, it is all much more complicated and just nutrition on its own is not enough. Just passing on mechanical knowledge is simply not fair.

Nutrition is very important, and I think it's a pillar of health, but there is more.

So, I've changed the way I work with my clients, and I realised I needed a voice on psychedelics. I can't just be some nutritionist talking about psychedelics, I need to have a master's where my thesis is based on psychedelics, psychedelics and live trauma. And that's what I'm working on now.

What effects does the connection with Nature have on your life?

Through the connection with Nature, I experience being more at peace, living in the moment, and feeling calm.

Why do you think modern society has lost its connection with Nature?

Modern society has lost its connection with Nature because we are abusing and destroying Nature, and have become very positivist in spirit, so we lack what Nature does with us.

We are obsessed with evidence and science, but what we don't understand is the tacit knowledge that we get from something like Nature. You can't really do a science experiment with Nature in itself. You can, but it's not going to give you any meaningful data. All that it might give you is something like, people who spend time in Nature are less depressed, for example.

It is like how you learn to play an instrument, how you would learn the notes on the sheet, and you know how to play a song, but the violinist isn't thinking about each individual note when he/she is playing, there's a degree of living and breathing the violin and learning. It is the same in Nature with how we know when we are experiencing the benefits of Nature, but we don't know how to comprehend or explain it. It's the same way with psychedelics, if you put the logic of a human mind on a psychedelic, it only goes so far as logic, which is what a human mind has created and that it's beyond our comprehension. And that's also what Nature is in a way, it has a cumulative effect on your health.

Thinking of nutrition - I'm a nutritionist after all – and the disconnection with Nature, I find it slightly oxymoronic, as nutrition should be around food, provided by Nature, but it is becoming very lab-coated, clinical, data driven and based on analytes. Lots of supplements are being recommended and people are forgetting the actual food element of nutrition and what it can essentially do for them, it's becoming more of a medicine. Allopathic medicine and even functional medicine are systems with methodologies attached, whereas Nature is a more than complex system.

Food is part of Nature, but there seems to be a superfood or a supplement for everything that is already naturally in food, so the more people could strip back to the actual food, the better.

The other issue is the dogma that we should be on some kind of diet, like Paleolithic, vegan, vegetarian and so on. Is this another control mechanism that will affect our health? We must look back; we have to look at how we have moved on. We are so obsessed with what we are being told we should be doing, rather than listening to our intuition and our own body to find out how we should eat, sleep and live.

In your opinion, what is the best way for people to get in tune with Nature?

Very simple, put your phone away and open your eyes, sit in a park and just be.

❧ Meet Daria & Heine – Founders of the Bliss & Stars Retreat in South Africa

After years of travelling and high-paced corporate careers in their home country Denmark, Daria Rasmussen and Heine Wieben thought it was time for a change. They discovered the importance of Nature and its innate power to impact positively on their mental and physical well-being. A change in lifestyle merged with time spent in Nature, looking up the night sky, and mindfulness practices is all it took.

Driven by lifelong passions to explore (human) Nature and valuable lessons learned from corporate careers and burnout, the idea of a transformational wilderness retreat was born.

They sold everything they owned and set off to South Africa to find their new home and a place for people to reset and turn towards a more wholesome and joyful life.

After months of searching, they found their home, on the banks of the Doring River, where they subsequently built their retreat.

Daria is a certified mindfulness teacher and holds a master's degree in sociology. She teaches what she has practiced over the years. Her guidance is rooted in ancient Buddhist tradition and modern neuropsychology and in the belief that mind, body, environment, food, and everything else we consume play the same parts in our wellbeing.

Heine is an astrophotography pro and Nature guide, who would like to share his fascination with astronomy and the cosmos, while immersing in Nature, to help people reconnect with themselves, satisfy curiosity, and find inner peace.

I was introduced to Daria and Heine by a friend, and I was fascinated by their story and intense connection with Nature. I had to find out more.

When did you start to connect with Nature?

For Daria, it goes back to her early childhood, because Nature was such a big part of her growing up. She grew up in Southern Poland and it was a family tradition to go for walks in the beautiful forests and sometimes they would drive to the mountains. Daria can still remember how majestic Nature was.

Heine grew up on a small island in Denmark with just 3,500 inhabitants, a small community. His parents had a butcher's shop on the island, but they sold that and bought a smallholding. Because it was on an island, the land they owned bordered the sea, so he also had the beach to play on, so lots of outdoor space to play.

Heine's granddad was a gardener and his parents loved gardening as well, so they had this huge vegetable garden, and they were more or less self-sufficient. Heine comes from a family that loves Nature and hunting. The family had a little cabin in the woods on a neighbouring island, and almost every weekend they would go there with his cousins and sometimes the adults would go out to hunt or just hang out, and the kids would play in the forest and go fishing in the lakes. The love of Nature has definitely been passed on by Heine's dad. When he was a young man, before he met Heine's mother, he went to North America, where he was riding the rodeo circuit, but for long periods of time he would take his rifle and fishing gear and would go off to the northern territories, northern Canada and Alaska, and just be in Nature.

Did you ever lose the connection and get out of tune with Nature?

Daria was a workaholic; she had a stressful job in marketing, and she suffered a burnout. This made her decide to get a dog, to get her out of the house, into Nature, even if it was a park: it made a huge difference to Daria's well-being.

Heine never really lost the connection with Nature despite being busy with his career in telecom and living in a big city (Copenhagen). He would just drive to the middle of nowhere to watch the night sky and take pictures. Also, he has always been a complete adrenaline junkie when it comes to the ocean, and he sees it as an important part of Nature. When he is out there in the waves, it is just him and Nature and he is totally in the moment. So, for Heine, the ocean and the night sky were his tools to stay sane in a busy office and living environment.

What happened next?

Heine started feeling as if he had been there and done that; he was getting tired of endless meetings and there were huge changes within the company, and he had to let go of a lot of staff members. Life is too short for things like that and because Heine really loves the night sky, Denmark was not the place to be any more, as Scandinavia is terribly overcast most of the time. Heine also needed some sunshine. So, he left his job. Daria and Heine had been talking about this before, but at the time they didn't have the courage. Now it was the right time.

Heine made it very clear that they didn't run away from something, but that they were running towards something, they just had to do something else. The way they were living was taking its toll on their health and their relationship, and they realised that they would regret it, if they would never try changing their life. The fact that they were both in their early forties and didn't have children made the decision to leave Denmark easier.

Travelling and Nature weren't new things for Heine and Daria, they have had it in their blood from early childhood. They just wanted to emphasise and share with people, in a tailored structure, the importance of Nature and its innate power to impact positively on mental and physical wellbeing.

After a lot of searching, they found somewhere in South Africa, where they settled, off the beaten track, about one hour 15 minutes off roading from the nearest gravel road. The land was completely untouched; nobody had lived there since the Bushmen. The location is a big part of what Daria and Heine are about, as there is a sense of peacefulness and calm.

Before Daria and Heine quit their jobs, they spent months driving around South Africa to see if it would feel right to move and they visited different properties that were for sale. They hooked up with some estate agents, just to get an idea of what was out there and what was possible.

The first time they visited the farm they couldn't find it initially. That's how remote it is.

Technically it is two farms on 1350 hectares, so quite a large plot of land, with a river running through. After four years, there are still areas of their land that they have to explore, because it's not flat, it is mountainous.

It was very different from what they had imagined. To start with, they had to build a 7-kilometre road for access. They arrived in their 4x4 car, with their belongings, a cool box and two paraffin lamps. Heine didn't even bring a toolbox. There was no running water or electricity, so it was quite a shock to the system, but they were amazed by the human capability to adapt and find a way, so it came very naturally. They couldn't Google, but just had to get on with things and find a way to do them.

Daria started with the vegetable garden, despite not having done any gardening before, but it came instinctively, as somehow, she knew what to do. Daria thinks that, as knowledge is stored in our DNA and hasn't changed since the early beginnings of mankind, this knowledge is probably encoded in who we are.

The first year there were many changes; their eating habits changed and even their bodies changed. It was not something they had planned; it all came naturally.

What effect(s) does your connection with Nature have on your life?

Pulling the vegetables out of the soil, seeing the seeds sprout, but also the raw beauty of Nature and overcoming their fear of snakes, etc. have made Daria and Heine feel in full harmony with Nature. And of course, the spectacular night skies, without any light pollution, have also brought them close to Nature. There is also a historical aspect to their life. On their land they have found nine rock art sites with cave paintings that are thousands of years old, making them feel that they're just there for a brief moment in time. The river valley with the old rocks, their formations shaped by the water and the wind, give them a sense of connection across time.

There is a true sense of belonging, a sense of home. Daria explained that she lost the sense of restlessness, of constantly wanting to go places. It is a feeling of oneness; of 'we are Nature'.

There is profound appreciation of life. Most people think that we have a million light years ahead of us, and there is time for everything. But Daria and Heine have this deep sense of how valuable and how miraculous it is to be alive, and how important it is to live in the moment.

Respect and gratitude are also a large part of their life. On paper they own the land, but they don't see themselves as landowners. Heine explained that he doesn't believe you can own land and he sees himself and Daria more as guardians, wanting to share the land with other people. It's a unique piece of land, totally unspoiled, and there are not many places in the world like that. The whole farm is a registered critical biosphere. Scientists found plants there that haven't been seen anywhere else on the planet and the river's ecosystem is home to several endangered fish species, so there is a sense of respect in conserving that and living in harmony with Nature without destruction.

It is a harsh environment and many of the plants are very old and have been struggling to survive. When they built on the land, they didn't want to uproot any plants, so most of the structures are built on stilts. The few exceptions are some stone buildings that had to have a foundation, but most of their structures are not invasive to the surroundings.

Why do you think modern society has lost its connection with Nature?

Modern society has lost its connection with Nature because of industrialisation. In Daria's view, we see Nature as something separate from us, something that can be dominated, used, and destroyed. Heine talked about the narrative of commoditisation and advertising, telling us that we need lots of stuff, and that is not exactly Nature speaking.

Heine and Daria were originally living in Copenhagen, and they had a lot of belongings, much more than they needed. When they sold their apartment, they packed most of their belongings in a container that didn't arrive in South Africa until much later and is still 75% packed. They realised that they didn't need that much, after arriving with three suitcases and two paraffin lamps.

In your opinion, what is the best way for people to get in tune with Nature?

People who come to the retreat are generally stressed and it's incredible to see what can happen in three days. There are many people who cry and say that they are feeling very much alive and begin to get a feeling of curiosity and joy for life. As Heine explained, it is a bit like when you are a child and you explore, without your parents. a new place where you have never been before. You get into a state of mind where you feel curiosity and awe.

The game changer at the retreat is that there is no Wi-Fi, and people don't use mobile phones, so they are more in the moment and see what's around them.

Once you surrender to Nature and embrace it, you actually feel held in the space, at least that is how Heine and Daria are feeling; they feel extremely safe where they are, even though they are far away from civilisation. They don't want to be anywhere else, and they are not worried at any given time about anything that could happen in Nature.

The best way to get in tune with Nature according to Daria and Heine is just to spend more time in Nature, go to a forest and surround yourself with greenery. It doesn't have to be all the way in South Africa, it can be anywhere. Even if you have a small backyard with just a piece of grass, on a warm summer night, put a blanket out there and try to sleep under the stars, you will feel closer to Nature.

Food can also bring you closer to Nature. Paying attention, having appreciation for what it takes to grow food, having a moment of reflection when you are eating - in all this Nature plays a huge role.

To grow some of your own food, you don't need to have a garden. Everybody has a window ledge, and you can grow microgreen, or put a small tomato plant in your window. Everyone can do that. And you can see how it will grow and with enough patience, you can have a small plate of food one day.

❧ Meet Ed – Botanist, Managing Director of Aquasol (botanicals) and Director of Bionutri Ltd.

Edward Joy grew up in Birmingham and spent much of his childhood in and around the health food shops owned by his father. Whether it was the dust of the herbs or the smell of vitamin pills, health foods became part of Ed's constitution, and he has worked in and around the health food trade since the early 1990's.

As a student, Ed trained as an illustrator, but after suffering a life-threatening illness in his early twenties he was brought back to many of the aspects of natural medicine to regain his health. During the 2 years he spent recovering, Ed studied Botany, Nutrition and Naturopathy.

In 2007 Ed helped his father Robert Joy to set up the naturopathic food supplements company Bionutri Ltd. When the company started to grow bigger, formulating more products to support the work of healthcare practitioners, Ed travelled across the UK and Ireland, speaking to groups of therapists, giving formal lectures and herb walks to help share an understanding of how people can heal themselves by reconnecting with Nature.

In 2019, pursuing his passion for herbalism, Edward established the botanicals company, Aquasol, producing a range of instant herbal beverages that offer all the benefits of herbs without the wastefulness of teabags or the use of additives.

In 2020, after the first national lockdown, Ed set up a weekly webinar to communicate with the thousands of practitioners who couldn't practice due to Covid. The webinars quickly became very popular and still run every Wednesday morning, presenting free talks on everything from herb walks to iridology, nutrition to naturopathy. This is how I met Ed and I can honestly say he is the most enthusiastic and knowledgeable lecturer I have come across in this field.

When did you start to connect with Nature?

I started to connect with Nature from a young age. Growing up in Birmingham, you connect to Nature in between the urban spaces, but there is no shortage of Nature, wherever you grow up. My earliest memories, when I was 9 or 10 years old, are of listening to the cuckoos, whilst poking around in the garden. It is striking to me, because I live in a much more rural area these days and I never hear cuckoos any more.

Thinking about the type of connection with Nature I had as a child, I suppose children don't really think about what they need. To me it was walking out of the house, to get away from my four brothers, my parents, and the dogs. As a child I didn't see it as an emotional connection, as I didn't recognise its necessity at the time. As an adult, reflecting on my behaviour as a child, I see it as walking away from the house to engage in the peace or tranquility. So, I think it was an emotional connection, but I wasn't aware of it, and I think it's only on reflection that I think perhaps it was absolute necessity.

Even growing up in a city, there was Nature, as Nature is all around you wherever you are. You can't hide it and you can't hide from it for very long. I used to do herb walks in London and one of the best places to do it was in London graveyards. It was the perfect place, and I would find wild plants in London that I have never seen in rural areas. In cities Nature is in corners and pockets and in a way for somebody living in a city, the experience is more intense.

Did you ever lose the connection and get out of tune with Nature?

In my view getting out of tune with Nature is a cycle we all get caught up in sometimes.

I did lose the connection too and got out of tune with Nature. I think the disconnection was caused by several factors, like a period of very poor health that I experienced in my early twenties. Low level infection, toxicity, stress, poor lifestyle choices, all of them could be described as a loss of connection.

What caused this disconnection?

In my late teens I was an artist, I studied Fine Art at university. I also spent a lot of time travelling.

When I was 20 years old, I was travelling in India and I was in a train crash, which was a very traumatic event. It was a horrific disaster and I had to be flown home from there.

Soon after that, and over the next year, I got into a cycle of poor health, partially due to a lot of alcohol, which is not untypical of a 20/21-year-old. I started to lose a lot of weight. I was down to about 9 ½ stone, being 6'1" tall. And I had started to develop these pains all throughout my body, but especially in my back and groin. It was something I ignored for a long time. I kept travelling and drinking, and then one day, on a walking holiday in the north of Wales, I became very, very ill and was brought home and X-rayed. It turned out that I had tumours all over my body, on my lungs, in my groin and my neck. It was something that had been growing for a long time, but I had been passing it off as a sports injury or a bad cough. It was about as bad as it could be.

So, I think that was a moment of reckoning, now 22 years ago. It was perhaps the major turning point in my life because it was one of the bleakest times that I can remember, but it was also, in many ways, very reassuring, because things could only get better. It was quite cathartic to think, now I must do something to improve my situation. And that was the point that I actually tended towards or turned to Nature. I did start with chemotherapy first, which was acutely effective, but it made me extremely unwell. The side effects hit me very hard, but it was extremely effective and within weeks I was experiencing big steps forward. I had these massive growths on my right lung, which, on an x-ray, looked like a kind of claw, holding on. As the chemotherapy went on, and they did more x-rays, the reduction of the mass was quite dramatic. My breathing improved a bit, but the pain was unbearable at times, a very deep sort of pain.

The chemotherapy made an enormous difference and was very effective, but it was so aggressive on my immune system, that I couldn't recover sufficiently, within the required timeframe, to add another dose, which is quite common. They couldn't carry on with the sort of chemotherapy that was necessary to make it effective. It started to make me think I was really in trouble, I really needed to think about something else. My parents and I asked my father's work colleague, who I still work with today, and who also had cancer 25 years earlier. He set about arranging a plan for me that could potentially help, involving some very strange and very peculiar ideas.

I was kind of au fait with alternative treatments. I grew up in a health food shop, and my father worked for a supplements company at the time. I do remember looking into chemotherapies and finding out that for instance for taxol chemotherapy, they use the bark from the yew tree. I was absolutely fascinated by the natural elements of these drugs.

I have to be honest, at the time I was quite a belligerent individual, and I wouldn't take anything, unless it was well explained to me. I said to my haematologist at the time, that I wanted to do everything I could to deal with this disease, but if could not accept it intellectually, I could not see how I could accept it physically. I wanted to know the what and the why. Luckily, my haematologist was open to the fact that I wanted to try alternative treatments too, and he understood if that was what I wanted to do, we needed to cooperate with each other. He obviously wanted me to keep the chemotherapy going and I did try. But instead of the twelve cycles for the full course, I only managed to do two. When I decided to stop, it was based on this need to do as much as I could to get rid of this cancer, but at the same time, doing as much as I could to live through the process.

How did you reconnect?

In the end, healing myself was a long, slow process, mostly taken up by reconnecting with Nature.

There was some herbal medicine involved and a lot of immunotherapeutic protocols. Vitamin C infusions were probably one of the major cruxes of that process. Three times a week my mother would drive me to a clinic in Leicestershire to have my intravenous vitamin C infusion. I was getting between 40 and 50 grams of vitamin C in a single infusion. I was also taking about 15 grams a day internally as well. And that was combined with using different mineral ascorbates of vitamin C.

My understanding of it, then and now, is that the vitamin C was being used because when we overdose on vitamin C, it forces nitrous oxide to run through the body and through the blood, which is very destabilising for cancer, which likes to form a protective sugary membrane around itself.

That was the first big immunotherapeutic treatment.

At that point I started studying botany, herbalism, and naturopathy. I had done some studying for many years before then, when I worked in a health food shop. Although I had formally studied fine arts, I had always kept the other studying going, and got a few accreditations in herbalism and nutrition. So, it was already part of my makeup at that time. I started to pursue it more seriously as I knew that whatever I was doing was going to be a long haul. And it was a very long haul, with vitamin C therapy, ozone therapy, Iscador therapy, which is mistletoe injections, an herbal preparation of the mistletoe plant, etc. I was under some form of clinical support for the next three years, but it worked. However, it will always be the shadow that is following me. I still think that I'm not actually out of the woods.

Occasionally, on a Friday evening, I'll treat myself to a beer. And I know if my godfather was with me, he would say, "Just make sure it's the one only." It is a lifetime of balance and I have accepted that for over 20 years now. I now feel that however we treat illness, in the end, to be healthy, a good nutritional constitution and a deep connection to Nature are the way to go.

What effects does the connection with Nature have on your life?

I work with herbs and nutrients. These to me are the factors that bind us to the natural world.

Part of my work is teaching health practitioners how to use herbs in their practice.

On a more personal level, I was told I would never have children because of the type of chemotherapy I was given. Nature had other plans. Just before I got married, my now wife was very keen to know if we could ever have children and two months later, she was pregnant.

Every day my son is a reminder of my triumph in overcoming cancer.

My son and I are very close, and we spend a lot of time together, because he is home-educated.

I am instilling a love of Nature in him, partially through the home-education.

At the moment, we are digging up comfrey roots and we are making comfrey oil. We will also be digging up nettle roots soon. He will be learning about the biochemistry of what is going on in a nettle root or a comfrey root, which is absolutely fascinating. Sharing that with him, on a level to which he can relate, is great. We also go in line skating together, which is quite an accident-rich sport. My son will bring his hypericum and calendula ointment with him, which he made himself.

When I am outside in Nature, I feel completely normal. I like to be away from the indoors. Away from the office, the house, from cars and roads. When I am not outdoors in Nature, I feel like I need something else. I need a cup of tea, I need a coffee, I need to call someone. But when I am outdoors, I do not need anything, and I love that feeling of tranquility. We find that really hard to grasp, actually being in an environment where you need nothing.

In 2006 after my illness, I went traveling in Spain. I spent a few months there, with my backpack and some paints, and eventually I found myself doing the Camino de Santiago. I got a bus to Roncesvalles on the Spanish border and started the Camino, walking every day on my own. It was the loveliest, most extraordinary experience I ever had, and I still look at it as one of the most enriching things that I have ever done. There is a community that you can engage with, someone to talk to, and I made some lifelong friends. But the most beautiful thing about that whole experience is not being there yet. The only thing you need to worry about is that you are not there yet. I found that to be the most powerful thing because everything else was about just walking and being outdoors.

I think, for me, it was perhaps an exercise in learning about my own Nature.

Why do you think modern society has lost its connection with Nature?

I think if we had really lost our connection to Nature, none of us would live for very long. However, I do think that if people were to understand how deeply Nature plays a part in their existence, it might make it easier for them to take better care of themselves and the world around them.

In your opinion, what is the best way for people to get in tune with Nature?

The most direct way for people to get in tune with Nature is through our diet. Not just what we eat, but how we eat and how we prepare our food. For me, shelling beans or peeling squash from the allotment, picking fruit from the garden or a hedgerow helps sustain a profound connection with Nature. Our rooting ground is what underpins it all.

We are transient beings, we do not fix our feet into the ground like the plants and the trees, we are always disconnected. Our engagement on that level is secondary. People think that when you eat something, it's gone, but it is not, it becomes internal, that food becomes a part of you.

We do not absorb the food that we eat, we absorb the products of the food and that to me helps me find affinity with everything else in Nature. It is the one thing, with all our distractions, that we have. It's the one thing that makes me see that actually we're just as natural as everything else.

🌿 Meet Élise – Biology Graduate and Traveller from Canada

Élise Candas was born in Paris, France and at the age of 6 she moved with her family to Canada. She grew up in Saint Boniface, a small French community in the city of Winnipeg. Élise attended the University of Manitoba where she recently graduated with a Major in biology, with a focus on plant science and botany.

She always knew she wanted to study biology and after her graduation, she started working as a research assistant for a master's project on poplar trees and their stress resistance.

After a year of working in a greenhouse and a laboratory, Élise spent the summer working as a gardener for Assiniboine Park Conservancy. In her spare time, she tends to her garden, growing lots of vegetables and herbs. During the summer she loves to cycle, hike, camp, and attend music festivals. In the winter, she has been playing ringette as goalie for more than 15 years. She also plays outdoor hockey with her friends or goes skating down the large river trail.

Just recently, Élise and her partner Nathan moved to Portugal for a year. They will be travelling and exploring, while also working. They are hoping to find any type of gardening job around the country. They also plan to visit Spain, Italy, and France where they will be able to spend time with Élise's grandma. Other than that, they will see where life will take them, as they are always up for another adventure.

When did you start to connect with Nature?

I started to connect with Nature at a very young age, about 5/6 years old, when I was living in France. We lived in Paris, in what was called 'la cité du béton', the concrete city. We had a neighbour, a very old lady called Madame Cabaret, who had a massive garden just beside us, and I used to go there quite often. It was very overgrown and there were vegetables, a big tree, and shrubs everywhere, and there were always these massive snails. I absolutely loved that place and really connected with it.

I also spent a lot of time with my grandma in the South of France. She had a beautiful, huge garden and we would go for walks almost every day, following a stream in Le Caloussu. These were beautiful Nature walks. I can still remember the Pins Parasol, which are tall pine trees that look like parasols. Those moments remind me of how connected I was to Nature then.

After we moved to Manitoba, Canada, I also connected with Nature, as I spent most of my summers at a cabin at Albert Beach. It was very important to me, because all my cousins would be there and we would be in the forest every single day, building forts, or at the beach, or we would be frog hunting.

I think, as a child, my relationship with Nature was a physical one, but also quite emotional. In Nature I felt happy and curious.

When I was a teenager, I still loved being outdoors. We had a trampoline in our garden, so we were always playing outside. But then the era of technology came, and we got a Wii which we all loved, and our friends would come over to play, so we weren't outdoors that much anymore. I think it all changed again when we realised that technology was growing and taking us away from Nature. So, later in my teenage years, my friends and I did a lot of camping, especially during the summer, and during the winter we did a lot of outdoor sports, like ice hockey.

I still do that with the same group of friends. We still go out for hikes here and there. We still go camping together, especially at the music festivals, and it's always fully outdoors.

My love for Nature made me decide to study biology. I started with animal studies, but after I took a term off to travel to South America with my partner, and having seen all the beautiful, lush greenery during our hikes, I felt that something was not fitting when I came back. So, I took some different courses and one of them was a plant anatomy course. I completely fell in love with that. We would go to the greenhouse, pick a plant, and dissect it and make microscope slides, which was just so beautiful. That class changed my whole route. I started taking all the plant courses that I could, focusing on plant physiology and plant science.

*Did you ever lose the connection and
get out of tune with Nature?*

I think that the most significant disconnection with Nature happened when I was a student, especially during the Covid pandemic. I was studying from home as all lectures were online, and I spent hours and hours on my laptop. I would wake up, turn on my laptop and not move from my desk, even though I was studying biology and plants, which is kind ironic. It was also a very harsh winter. It was definitely the time where I felt out of tune with Nature.

The wait, not being able to use our laboratories and not even hands-on work with the plants; I was missing and craving Nature.

How did you reconnect?

As soon as I finished my studies, I closed my laptop, and started gardening a lot.

I made my own garden bed, started planting and seeding, and just went a bit crazy with it.

It was such good fun. I also started cycling a lot and helped my dad with his garden, spending as much time outdoors as possible.

And then I got lucky, as I started a job as a research assistant for a master's project in a plant physiology laboratory. I spent most of my time in a greenhouse, surrounded by poplar trees.

I also spent a summer as a gardener at Assiniboine Park Conservancy in Winnipeg.

That is where I found that reconnection with Nature again.

*What effects does the connection with
Nature have on your life?*

I think the connection with Nature not only brings me happiness and pure joy, but it also brings me soothing and calmness. It's quite therapeutic. I love having my hands in the dirt and being outside all the time, I think it is great for my mental health.

Especially when I am gardening, it's just having the time to think and have this kind of pause in my life, where it's just me and my garden, with my thoughts.

The connection with Nature is one of the most important things for me; Nature is where I feel most comfortable and at peace. I feel strongest and most confident in Nature, and I feel really one with the world and part of the ecosystem. Humans or trees, we're just in a different composition of elements.

There is also a spiritual effect sometimes. Like when we were travelling in South America, and we got to the top of a mountain, at a very high altitude, and there was this blue lagoon. We felt this wave of energy, almost like ecstasy. It was a truly beautiful moment.

Why do you think modern society has lost its connection with Nature?

I think modern society has lost its connection with Nature because of the rise of technology, which I have seen happening in my generation.

We were outdoors all the time when we were young, but when the Wii came that changed a lot. Then the technology of mobile phones, iPads and new video games arrived, and it took people even more away from Nature. Obviously, we got a lot of good out of technology, but I think that we need to find a balance and some sort of moderation.

Another issue is the lifestyle of our modern society; that fast-paced lifestyle. We have got to go to work, we have got to go back home, do those chores, and I don't think Nature comes as a priority anymore. We always have something to do and are always so busy with work, studies, etc.

However, I think that during Covid when people had time to go for a walk or into their garden, there was some reconnection with Nature, but now there are a lot of people working from home and a lot of offices have closed. People are mixing work life with home life and there is almost no separation so if you're not taking breaks or forcing yourself to go out for a walk, you get trapped in that scenario.

In your opinion, what is the best way for people to get in tune with Nature?

The best way to get in tune with Nature is to try to get yourself to step outside your house or your office. If you have the privilege of being able to go for a walk in a natural habitat, if you have a forest nearby, a wetland or prairie, that is great, but of course that's not the case for everyone. Sometimes just going around your neighbourhood, looking at the trees and using your senses is already enough to connect.

I always do that; I always try to touch the leaves of a bush or feel the bark and look how the branches form on a tree or smell the flowers. There is Nature everywhere, even if you live in the deep depths of a city that's full of concrete everywhere. There are trees here and there. Just take the time and pause. When I see something beautiful, I take a pause, take three deep breaths, and take a moment.

When you go for a walk, take a little magnifying glass, as it's so neat to go look at mosses and other natural things. Even a blade of grass is interesting. It doesn't take much effort to do this.

For some people a walk might be too much because they are not able to walk or just can't find the time. You can also bring Nature into your house or office by buying an indoor plant to bring a little bit of green, a bit of Nature to you. I remember when I studied, I started buying a lot of plants for my house, I almost had a full indoor garden with about 80 plants.

Growing your own vegetables and herbs is a good way to connect with Nature. Although in Canada we don't have a long growing season. But you can always grow things indoors.

It's quite simple.

❧ Meet Emily – Forager and Documentary Producer

Emily Smith is 29 years old and lives in Peckham, South London with her little Greek street dog Apollo. Her dad is English, with Welsh/German heritage, and her mum was born in Japan of Korean parents.

Emily lived in London until she was 3 years old, when they moved to the countryside. She then moved to a town at 13. She has always been a dreamer and despite having huge amounts of energy and thriving off human connection, she also likes to enjoy the slower things in life. Nothing fills her with joy more than the tenderness of a simple home-cooked meal for someone you love (this can include herself!). Foraging has combined so many wonderful passions; cooking, walking, appreciating and celebrating Nature, preserving (both physically and metaphorically), learning about myths and traditions, and forming deep connections with people and other organisms.

I have been in awe of Emily's foraging skills and her cooking. She is so in tune with Nature, a true inspiration. You can follow her foraging finds and what she cooks with them on Instagram @down2forage.

When did you start to connect with Nature?

I grew up in the countryside and spent lots of time on my own with my dog, examining plants and poring over books. Many of my early-life memories are connected with the natural world.

The feel of the different seeds of grass, that I used to pull off as I walked, or the cool shiny smoothness of the horse chestnut. Being covered in morning dew, lying amongst the snowdrops. The scent of freshly cut grass, or piles of damp, rotting leaves. I got stuck up the old oak tree for hours.

I experienced the reality of living in the countryside with parents, who were strict about me helping with the garden chores. Raking up leaves never filled me with as much joy as planting seeds in spring and watching them grow. My pocket money would be granted after filling a wheelbarrow with sticks to pile onto a bonfire, where jacket potatoes would be roasting for that evening's meal.

An avid reader, by age four I first read 'Anne of Green Gables' and I would read the series again and again throughout my childhood. My mother had read these books as a child herself, and it had such an impact on her that she gave her daughter, me, the middle name Anne! Anne, the sensitive and imaginative heroine has a deep appreciation of the beauty of Nature that became interwoven in my life and my feelings. This cultivated a very poetic, whimsical, spiritual, and emotional connection with Nature.

My parents also instilled the love for Nature in me, in small ways that I didn't appreciate until I was an adult. They first taught me how to really 'see' what was in front of me. For example, my mother taking in the fragrance of a blooming flower. My dad kneeling before another bud and then their discussion of the comparison of the sweet aromas.

My dad would suddenly stop the car on country lanes and hoist me onto his shoulders to gather bags of damsons, cobnuts, or apples, often spotted whilst driving. He would complain that the squirrels always got to the beech nuts before us. I have fond memories of the annual freezing cold sloe collection which involved the whole family. Even my brother, who was four years older and much less into the outdoors, would join.

I now realise that much of my attitude to Nature has been influenced by my mum's background. I'm sure it has affected my gratitude. In Japan, a respect and love of Nature is unconditional. The culture encourages humans to coexist in harmony with it. And living in a household where nothing ever gets wasted means I have inherited this frugality!

Did you ever lose the connection and get out of tune with Nature?

We left the countryside when I was 13 years old and moved to a town. As a teenager, I became distracted by music, boys, and drinking. I had a few precious occasions where I reconnected with Nature, like wild swimming in a river near my friend's house in the summer, but these were far and few between.

However, there was always something missing. I felt lost and alienated but I couldn't put my finger on why. I never understood why I didn't seem to enjoy the same things that my friends did. I particularly hated staying out late and binge drinking but didn't understand that I could opt out of it.

What caused this disconnection?

I believe that the disconnection was caused by my attempts to conform and fit in. It took me many years to acknowledge that I have always felt different, and that is OK. I've learned to do things on my own. And even though my friends may be different from me in many ways, I still love them.

How did you reconnect?

When Covid struck, I had just returned from filming a full-on documentary with the police in Kansas City - going to murders of children by children. Before that, I had broken off a serious relationship, so I had nowhere to live. I got stuck living at my parents' house for the first time since I was a teenager. I began walking long distances, which I never thought I would be able to do as I have joint hypermobility.

The reconnection really took on new legs when I started foraging, which happened organically. Being highly food motivated, I spent a lot of time cooking. I spotted a huge patch of wild garlic and then added it to every meal. Something in my brain clicked, and I began studying in earnest. I realised that I also had secret knowledge in my subconscious from books I had examined in childhood.

Since the pandemic, life has been far more flexible, and this has been such a good thing for me. I'm away half the year filming, working intense 16-hour days. The rest of the time I'm editing or working on pre-production. Now I am usually able to work from home most days, so I can manage my own time. It means I take a very long walk and find my lunch!

What effects does the connection with Nature have on your life?

Reconnecting with Nature feels like a return to a dormant state inside of me, that has been waiting to be awoken. My awakening has brought so much joy to my life. I have cultivated a passion for walking. Walking everywhere fills me with joy - I'm spotting plants, keeping fit, saving money and being environmentally friendly. I'll walk across the whole of London to meet a friend - I just leave earlier and enjoy the journey. My friends get mad because I will do anything to avoid getting a taxi!

I have gained so much self-confidence - I realise that the possibilities are endless. I am more conscious of my surroundings. I really try to breathe it all in. Slowing down and breathing deeply was not something I could do before. I am always multitasking, doing ten things at once, suffering from undiagnosed ADHD my whole life. The best part of my job is people-facing and I always struggled with sitting in an office at a computer. A two-hour walk in the morning helps me feel more focused. I can sit at a desk and tackle menial tasks with a new kind of calmness, and I don't feel like I've wasted my morning.

The pleasure I get from Nature is not just limited to being in the woods. I live in London, and people are always surprised that I choose to live there and can forage. I remind them that Nature prevails. There is beauty here too. Wild places that are away from exhaust pipes and fumes, where I gather my lunch. I smile when I see a Hart's-tongue fern pushing its way through a wall on Oxford Street. I notice the leaves blowing in the wind. It is all about this new 'seeing.'

Foraging has helped me understand the passage of time - each month a different plant or mushroom is available. Blink and you might miss something!

It has also emphasised that food should not be taken for granted. The vegetables and fruits we consider 'normal' have been bred. Other species are completely overlooked and labelled 'weeds'. Broccoli, cabbage, Brussels sprouts, cauliflower... even kohlrabi are members of the Brassica family and were cultivated by humans from wild cabbage. All members of the Brassica family are edible, and I come across many on my forays! And they can taste even better than the cultivated ones.

There are so many wild alternatives, whereas species in the supermarkets have become homogeneous. There is no reason to buy spinach when I can find fat hen, tree spinach, dead nettles, nettles, dandelion, ground elder, cleavers, clover, chickweed, mallow… the list goes on!

The modern world has forgotten, but they are abundant, delicious, and very good for you. Our ancestors enjoyed these plants for their nutritional value, flavour and medicinal benefits!

There are also sustainable and ethical viewpoints. If you forage responsibly, you can reduce your carbon footprint, in combination with shopping locally and eating seasonally wherever possible.

Why do you think modern society has lost its connection with Nature?

There are many burdens in modern life. You cannot see what's right in front of you if you are staring at your phone. With so many toxic illusions forced down our throats, is it any wonder that modern society is disconnected with Nature? My least favourite illusion / delusion is the idea that your hustle leads to happiness. I hope one legacy of Covid remains - a fight to redress work life balance. I'm an avid supporter of a four-day work week.

I also resent how much cars dictate our lives. Of course, I'm very aware of how they have broadened our horizons. But as someone who's never owned a car, I find it frustrating how dominant car culture can be.

When it comes to food, as in so many facets of life, people expect instant gratification with little thought as to where the food comes from. So many don't blink an eyelid about ordering several takeaways a week delivered lukewarm on a motorbike, or their groceries arriving the same way.

There is a lack of education about where food comes from and first and foremost there should be a move to integrate food sovereignty into government policy. Secondly, there should be more incentive and encouragement for people to shop seasonally, locally, and to cut down on food waste. Thirdly, children at school should be educated about food and spend time in Nature.

There are so many reasons why modern society has lost connection with Nature... Individualism and narcissism in society, a breakdown of community, globalisation, mass consumerism… the list goes on.

In your opinion, what is the best way for people to get in tune with Nature?

The best way for people to get in tune with Nature is to realise you are a part of it. Being amongst trees that were here hundreds of years before you, and will outlive you, allows perspective. It's easy to be weighed down by modern life. I understand that not everyone has the luxury or privilege to be able to teach themselves to forage (safely). It's more through respect and appreciation of Nature that one's attitude towards food and general well-being can be improved.

Mushrooms can save your life! And this isn't even touching on the recent research that fungi could actually save the world from our human created problems. There is something wonderful in that unknown. I need to be hopeful.

There is a Japanese concept - shinrin yoku, which is forest bathing. Doctors prescribe it as a remedy for urban life and the benefits are documented. Even today, Western medicine treats symptoms rather than the overall health and happiness of the individual. My motto is prevention is better than cure.

The funny thing is that when you start 'looking', you can spot things everywhere. Like the Baader-Meinhof phenomenon. Our brains are so overstimulated and have developed a sort of override for 'unnecessary' information. That means we are conditioned not to notice. My friends are all shocked the first time we are walking together in London, and I point out edible plants and fungi in the pavement cracks. The same friends will go on to send me pictures of mushrooms spotted on their own, saying, 'I had never seen a mushroom in the wild before!' I tell them, they've been there the whole time waiting for you to see them.

For me, foraging is not just a means to an end. One of the things I appreciate most about identifying mushrooms is that it takes two hands. When you first come across the fungus there is a moment when you bend down to look closer, to smell it and closely examine it with your fingers.

I have learned patience, and to enjoy time spent outside without expectations. I have formed a new community with like-minded individuals. I have a new mindset. I love learning about all plants and examining them. It is not just about grabbing some leaves and throwing them into your bag. Often, I will just observe. I see it as embarking on a vow of trust. Leave no trace and take only what you need.

If we slow down, open our eyes, and admire what is in front of us, maybe then we would be less inclined to destroy it.

🌿 Meet Fred – Agro-ecological Farmer

Fred Price is an agro-ecological farmer, who, supported by his family, looks after Gothelney Farm, a small family farm at the foot of the Quantock hills in Somerset. His mother Victoria grew up on the farm. From the 1980s her sister Caroline cared for the farm through a challenging period. Today Fred continues the farming story, producing pork and grain.

For 12 years they have been transitioning the farm to agroecology, the application of ecological concepts and principals in farming, reimaging a new small farm future, where a farm feeds people justly, rather than via an extractive, cumbersome and commodified food system.

Earning the right to farm without inputs means considering the soil as a vibrant, living ecosystem. Their rotation reflects a need to prime the soil with enough carbon (foodstuff of bacteria, protozoa, and microbes at the base of the soil food web) and care for beneficial insects and microbes that build a resilient low-input farming system.

Gothelney Farm is about growing nourishing food, providing enriching jobs and a deep love of their biosphere.

I have been following Fred on Instagram for quite a while and I was blown away by how he works his farm. The fact that the farm also hosts Rosy Benson's bakery, made it even more interesting for me as a nutritional therapist, as they offer workshops on the use of diverse regional grains.

Agro-ecological farming and the connection with Nature are strongly entwined, that's why I would like to share Fred's story with you.

When did you start to connect with Nature?

Until I was 18 years old, I lived in London, but I always visited Gothelney Farm in Somerset, as it was my mother's family farm. There was one chap called Gerald, who spanned the generations, he worked for my great-grandfather, my grandfather, my aunt, and he was still working on the farm after I left university. Gerald had a very profound effect on me. We were friends, family really. Thinking back now it is so sad that all his reflections were stories of how the farm was when he was my age, full of fun and people. It makes me sad to see he hasn't lived to see the farm now. He taught me to "think of the farm like a garden" and had the most wonderful attitude – every day was a new day, as he used to say, "the world goes on, the birds still sing". I think that reflects the kind of resilience you need as a grower.

Thinking of my childhood, I have many pictures and memories from being at the farm. When I was 12 or 13 years old, I would come down here instead of going on holiday with my family. Now my whole family lives here, they've all gradually started moving back, which I think is a reflection of how the farm is changing.

I think growing up in London gave me a wonderful perspective on life being diverse, which I don't think I would have got if I grew up here. Some aspects of farming are sort of innate, you can't really go and study them or be taught, you just have to absorb them. If you are a child growing up on a farm, you more or less learn how farming is done. Living in London as a child meant I lost out on that, particularly when it comes to animal husbandry. On the other hand, it meant that I didn't have any blinkers on and there was not too much inertia in terms of how I saw the farm and how I saw the world. Which is why looking back, it always surprises me that the first five years of working at the farm, I did it the 'industrial' way despite not having gone to agricultural college and not having been taught about it. I just didn't question it.

My connection with Nature as a child was not really just about being outdoors. I think it was more about purpose. I had a real sense of doing and interaction from a food point of view, like growing vegetables and garden plants, it was much more fun. It was, in a way, about what is the function of Nature, and it evolved from there, to what we were using Nature for, like how we could grow crops and what interactions that would entail. It was coming almost full circle to that childhood thing of just being part of Nature. It made me feel happy, but then I went through a more or less egocentric phase from my late teens into my late 20s.

When I was younger it was a very individual interaction, but now I can't separate it from people. I think all the people that are a part of this zoomed out version of the farm, were what's enabled me to change my farming practices and hence make me feel different about Nature and my connection to the land; it is actually a kind of socio economy. The people that have been part of the journey of the farm and reimagining our food system are fundamental, so it's a collectively created personal feeling.

I would say that for the last five or six years, I think I've been much more mindful of my place in Nature, which in a way is the same as how it was at the beginning, I just wasn't aware of it. I think how I feel now when I'm outside, is probably the truest sense of how I was when I was an innocent child, being outside on the farm. I am just a bit more conscious of it now. I suppose since I started farming, I have been connected with Nature in a very direct way.

Did you ever lose the connection and get out of tune with Nature?

We always spent a lot of time at the farm, it was a place for the family to come together on the weekends and holidays. I always wanted to farm. Out of all my cousins who lived there, I was the only one that was really getting stuck in outside. I can't really explain it, there was something inside of me that knew this was what excited me and what I wanted to do.

During my teenage years, farming was very strongly associated with being here, but when I went to university to study geography, I realised that farming wasn't just connected to the place and the people there. I realised that it was what I needed to do with my life. Farming encompasses so many different things, and studying geography, I got the ability to see how things are connected and the impact that has. Given my mentality and my personality, I need to create narratives in my head to understand things and they may be very simplistic, but they give me purpose, and they give me a point to every single action now, no matter how small.

I think, with hindsight, my connection with Nature has always been there but it has changed over the past 15 years.

What caused this disconnection?

Looking back, the first 5 years of farming, I was very much following the industry norms.

We were an arable farm growing commodity crops (wheat, oilseeds, barley, maize, etc. but it may very well have been milk, pigs, or poultry). In that system we weren't in control of our destiny in any respect, particularly economically. With no control over price, the farmer leans towards scale and yield to keep one's head above water. I was no exception. This inevitably creates an addiction to synthetic products - to manage big, simple operations, which are therefore vulnerable, and to 'outyield' our environment by applying various agrochemical inputs. I suppose what I'm trying to say is that the disconnection was a result of big socio-economic forces - our food system, rather than any inbuilt desire to farm in a nasty way!

How did you reconnect?

I reconnected with Nature by rethinking how our food system works. I could begin to rediscover a farming system that didn't try and submit an environment to its will, but rather feel for a kind of balance, of taking and giving.

I wouldn't go as far as to say we are farming in harmony with Nature because that would imply perfection, I think it's an ongoing process. When you think you've got it worked out, you're about to make a big mistake. Farming is a very real thing, if you do something you know about it, as your interaction is manifested in a big way. Either in stock, soil, or crop, you can't deny it, you can't unsee it.

Every daily task, from the small things to the big strategic thinking is all through the lens of, 'What would Nature do?', 'How does Nature operate? Because Nature is the most productive, resilient, highly functioning ecosystem there is, looking at the human ecosystem that the farm is, and the economy within which the farm is operating, why wouldn't we want to copy and take inspiration from those logics that operate in natural ecosystems?

We are continually learning, and when you exert to make a change on the farm, there is always a response. The equilibrium moves when you make a change, and therefore there will be another change that becomes obvious to you or another opportunity to make change. So, it's inevitably a continuous process.

What effects does your connection with Nature have on your life?

My daily work is now full of life-affirming and positive activities - rather than trying to kill, suppress, or pre-empt disaster, we are fostering healthy, vibrant soils and ecosystems. This is important on a day-to-day basis, but also in the bigger picture - farming is going to have ups and downs, being able to 'weather' those is all about your state of mind. So, feeling that successes and failures, regardless of the seasons, overall, the piece of the world I'm responsible for is better than it was 12 months ago, is a safe thought to fall back on in those tired, low moments.

My connection with Nature, especially through farming, has beneficial effects on my physical and mental health. Physically, I consider myself very active and fit and that feels good. Mentally, immersing myself in the day to day, ritualistic routines of farming, make me calmer, see things more clearly and have a good perspective, especially when I'm feeling anxious about running a business and all the different aspects of that, or anxious about what is going on in the world, or with my family.

Why do you think modern society has lost its connection with Nature?

The way agriculture is practised, is big, commodified, globalised and industrialised, it's a machine that's operating, and in that system there's a big disconnect between someone eating food and someone growing it, to the point where farmers don't consider themselves food producers, and I speak from personal experience.

Everything is just a widget. If you're growing wheat, you get a contract, a passport for the grain, everything is depersonalised and dehumanised. And the way you sell it is you have a trader, and often the traders are trading five, six times before the actual physical commodity is moved. And even when it's moved, it's just a commodity. You don't even know where it's going sometimes. Every aspect of it is dehumanised and therefore you don't consider yourself growing food, which totally changes your interaction with the whole system. And similarly, from the perspective of a consumer going to a supermarket, it is completely disconnected. A good example is the branding of food now as plant based. I picked up a bag of lentils the other day and it was labelled as plant based. How disconnected are we when we have to inform people that lentils come from a plant!!

Considering food is the one moment in the day in our modern, technological, and highly urbanised society, where anyone can have a direct connection with Nature and Nature-based farming, but the problem is that there are industrial farming systems that are far removed from Nature. The reason why the industrial system is removed from Nature, is because it's trying to impose itself on a natural system, because they trade food as a commodity, rather than ecological farming systems, which try and read the context, and then reflect their practices to that context.

So, when you trade food as a commodity, the price of the commodity has no bearing on the cost of production in Somerset or Nigeria or Kazakhstan or wherever. It's a globally determined price and the farmer has certain ways of being profitable. You can get a very big farm, because then you reduce your costs per acre, and therefore you can stay profitable. However, the problem is when you have a big farm, you have to simplify the system, and simple systems aren't resilient. And therefore, you must manage all these vagaries of Nature and eliminate all the complexity, and use chemical, synthetic products. That is the industrial farming system - big, commoditised and with no true cost accounting in the food system.

It is not enough just to trust farmers to be connected to Nature and to reimagine their farming systems. You can't have an ecologically minded, Nature-based system of farming that's producing food in the same way as the industrial system, because it will never match up, it's not compatible.

So, I think food is the one aspect where we can really tackle all these high-level problems without having to address them directly just to get food right in a simple, connected, agroecological way.

We must believe that change is possible. I've become much more realistic and pragmatic about what that change looks like and I think it is OK if change makes the whole system 1% less bad, as that is moving in the right direction.

I trust in systems, which probably goes back to my geography degree and understanding of systems. You need a tipping point. At the moment supermarkets might have a 95% market share of how food is produced in the UK, and organic might only have a 5% market share, but there are thresholds. Hence, we might only need to get the small food system up to 10-15% and then the whole model of the industrialised big food systems comes crashing down, because they might need a certain scale and volume to maintain efficiencies.

Covid showed us how non-resilient the big food system was and at the moment there is the short supply of certain fruits and vegetables and empty shelves in the supermarkets, while in my organic vegetable box I still get the same stuff every week that I had last year and even five years ago.

It is good to understand the way supermarket contracts work with minimum quantities on a supply contract. Supermarkets have a monopolising grip on pricing for farmers, so the farmers will supply the minimum to fulfill the contract and then they'll sell the rest to Europe, because they get better prices. So, a lot of produce grown in the UK is actually being exported to Europe.

In your opinion, what is the best way for people to get in tune with Nature?

The best way for people to connect with Nature is through food. In simple terms, by asking yourself the question, where is my food coming from? A whole lot of other questions will probably crop up that will lead you to developing an understanding of how food is grown and Nature.

I think if you described conventional farming to people, alongside, for instance, organic farming, people would inevitably rather buy organic produce. But the access to this kind of food system is deeply problematic, and I don't have all the answers. But I also refuse to be criticised for believing that it should be our dominant food system. Just because the dysfunctional, conventional system is accessible to people doesn't make it right. We must stop criticising ecological, organic farming systems for being inaccessible and start working out how to make them accessible, and also to point out the true cost of the conventional food system. However, there is a lot of radical political and economic change that would need to happen to make that possible, but nevertheless, that is not a reason to not do it and not believe in it.

Conversations on the Lost Connection with Nature

From a Nature point of view, when the connection with Nature is lost, calling Nature 'Nature', or saying you need to connect to Nature would be quite inaccessible and potentially scary if you are disconnected from it because of your life experience or current place in the world. But there is always hope, as Nature is not a sexy marketing narrative that has been created. Nature is very real, it is about the most real and undeniable thing that it can be, despite all our impact on it, it still exerts an influence on us. So that's why there will always be hope, as it will always be pushing back in an equal and opposite direction, it will always be trying to find a balance and equilibrium. It's Nature's laws, it is above us and beyond us, and it is in our power to pick up that connection again if it is lost.

❧ Meet Guy – Organic Farmer, Founder of Riverford - an organic farm and organic vegetable box delivery company, and 'self-confessed veg nerd'

Guy Singh-Watson was brought up on Riverford Farm, in Devon. He studied Agricultural and Forestry Science at the University of Oxford. After university Guy worked on the family farm for a couple of years and then became a management consultant in London. He was asked to set up an office in New York. After just two years he handed in his notice and became a sailing instructor in Maine. After a while he came back to the UK and in 1986, he started growing organic vegetables on the family farm, with the idea of shortening the food chain and supporting the connection between producers, consumers and what's on their plate.

In 2018 Guy sold 74% of Riverford to its employees, at about one third of the market value.

In May 2023 he announced to sell out the rest of his shares and Riverford will become 100% owned by its staff. Guy is not going to retire just yet, but he will continue to be involved in the business as a trustee, non-executive director, and spokesperson

Guy's story is about sustainable food production, being an ethical business that is commercially effective, and farming in harmony with Nature.

When did you start to connect with Nature?

I grew up on Riverford Farm in Devon, where I was helping out on the farm from a very early age, starting with mucking out the pigs and collecting eggs.

Undoubtedly, I was very connected to Nature, but I think perhaps in a sort of very physical or functional way. I certainly wasn't conscious, even in retrospect, of any spiritual connection with Nature. I was out there, every hour that I could, and it was where I wanted to be.

I knew the farm. As a matter of fact, I knew the farm better, physically, as a five-year-old than I do as a sixty-year-old now. Even though my legs were very short, I knew every tree, every hole in every hedge, where I could get through. It was very functional.

It wasn't a simple, direct love of Nature or anything. I'm not going to pretend that at all.

It is probably different now, but not when I was growing up, but I'm sure I was very happy, and it was where I felt my happiest.

I was a bit of a loner as a child. Maybe that was the result of growing up on a farm, but anyway, I would go out and about around the farm, mostly on my own. And that was where I felt comfortable. And I thought it was where I felt happy. But when I got to my forties, I had to concede to myself that I am actually not a loner at all, and that human company is incredibly important to me. I do not need very much of it, but if I do not have any of it, I am essentially rather poor at being on my own. It was during a trip to New Zealand, while being in the absolute wilderness, that I could not wait to get back to the city, despite not being a city person. I just wanted to be surrounded by people.

Did you ever lose the connection and get out of tune with Nature?

Yes, I did when I was working in London and New York for a couple of years.

I did have a really good time in New York, but I did feel quite disconnected. I was miserable in London; I really was a fish out of water. I was not conscious of the fact that I could not be happy in that environment, but I somehow knew that I just had to get back to the farm, it was something visceral. London just did not suit me at all, in many ways. I love cities and towns but for relatively brief periods. I think cities are an incredible testimony to our ability to live together and cooperate with each other. We are not savages at all, contrary to the belief of our current government.

What caused this disconnection?

I was not in the right place for me, it was not feeding me.

How did you reconnect?

I reconnected with Nature again by coming back to Devon.

I love the sea and when I have a chance I go to quite extreme places, where other people don't go. I will lower myself down a cliff with a rope, go and jump off a rock or something, because I just like being on my own. Being part of Nature.

Sailing is another connection to Nature for me. There is a motor in my boat, but I just use it to get in and out of the harbour. I want to be part of Nature and I just do not understand people who chase around in power boats, being in a rush to get somewhere. They are not participating in anything. I just do not get it at all.

What effects does the connection with Nature have on your life?

Just being part of it forces me to slow down a bit. It is similar when I am farming and being part of the landscape, interacting with it, shaping it, but also learning from it.

I enjoy being part of it.

I do not really want to dominate Nature. When I bring in a swing shovel and build a reservoir or something, it actually distresses me that I am tearing the soil apart. I do not like that, but when it is finished and it fills with water and things start growing on it after a year or two, I am enjoying it.

The way I was brought up was that you always had to try to do something useful and not indulge yourself. I suppose part of that was being out there and enjoying it. Growing food works very well for me, I do need a tangible purpose for most things that I do.

I take being connected with Nature through growing vegetables for granted. And so do all my family, because it's what we've always done, it has always been there.

My enthusiasm for cooking normally comes from being out there and picking something, and as I'm picking, I'm thinking how I am going to cook it.

You would be surprised at how unconnected some farmers are. Farming becomes very functional. Most if it is obviously very mechanised these days. It is a bit shocking to see how disconnected the modern farming world has become from Nature, unfortunately, with environmental problems as a result. This is a challenge we are going to have as we need to get farmers on board to change this.

As a farmer, you spend a lot of time essentially destroying Nature. It is not just spraying glyphosate; even ploughing a field, or cutting a hedge are destructive acts.

Some farmers have convinced themselves that keeping the farm neat and tidy is what being a custodian of the land is all about. Quite often, a lot of those practices are quite damaging. However, they are people that have the skills to farm in a different way. So, we really need to get them on board.

Luckily there are still lots of younger people who are interested in farming, and particularly regenerative farming, people who do want to farm in a different way. There is lots of hope in the new generation.

I once said, "Being in the field with my vegetables recharges me".

Some people assume I'm an extrovert, because I can get up on a stage and give a talk and even be mildly amusing sometimes, but I'm most definitely an introvert. My definition of an introvert is where you go to recharge your batteries. I want to be on my own, even though I have come to appreciate that I do not want to be on my own all the time. But if I'm tired or stressed, or I just can't cope with things, I just want to go to the field.

Why do you think modern society has lost its connection with Nature?

Well, I do think food has a lot to do with it.

Globally 50% of people are probably engaged in producing food in one way or another.

The connection with Nature comes from the connection with the seasons, where you can only do certain things at certain times of the year, only eat certain things at certain times a year. To my mind, there's nothing more soulful than foraging for mushrooms in autumn, or what I really love doing is picking up softshell clams in winter, when it is safe to eat them. When I do that, I feel very connected with Nature.

The same counts for picking things in my fields, but probably a bit less so. So yes, I think that is the root of the connection with Nature and there are clearly so few people engaged with that, other than the people who are growing a small number of vegetables in their gardens and get their hands in the soil. They have as much connection as a farmer who grows 100 acres of vegetables and rarely gets out of his tractor cabin.

For some people the connection with Nature can come through birdwatching, for others it is geology or the ocean. So, why have we lost it? Because we live such unnatural lives, especially recently with the digital revolution and spending more and more time indoors.

Food retailing and marketing generally have a lot to do with it. You go into a supermarket, and you have no idea what time of year it is. Everything looks very aesthetic and uniform, maybe a bit less cellophane nowadays, but still unnatural. A retailing method that is all food processing industry. In this country 50% of the food we eat is ultra-processed. It has lost any connection to anything natural and that is awful for our health and awful for the environment, but unfortunately really cheap. We do not actually touch the real stuff. We have so little connection with Nature through being in it or even handling it in our kitchen.

The food retailing system, the amount of money spent on promoting ultra-processed food, sweet drinks, etc. would be a hundred times the amount spent on any campaign to get people to eat vegetables.

Vegetables used to be cheap, even organic vegetables, relative to processed food. But the less people eat of them, the more it becomes a self-fulfilling prophecy. Vegetables have become substantially more expensive relative to other foods because they don't lend themselves to this sort of mechanisation process so well. If you're just paying for calories, processed food is the cheapest way of getting them, unfortunately.

*In your opinion, what is the best way for
people to get in tune with Nature?*

If you really get connected with Nature, if you farm organically anywhere, or if you work in your garden, you must learn a degree of humility, because it does go wrong sometimes. You are not the master of everything. And you know what goes wrong, and it's not the end of the world. There is the sort of humility that comes from just being, even if you're out and you get soaked in the rain, and you're not in control of your destiny for a minute. That is not a bad thing to experience really.

Connect with the seasons (and eat seasonally), spend more time outdoors and try to be part of Nature by just being. And eat vegetables! Preferably organic.

✒ Meet Jenny – Medical doctor, Author, Lecturer and Broadcaster

Jenny Goodman qualified at Leeds University Medical School in 1982, and worked as a junior doctor in General Medicine, Surgery and A&E. Disillusioned with conventional medicine's inability to heal sick people, and its failure to enquire about the causes of illness or to do preventive healthcare, she left. She then lectured extensively, both on medical sciences to practitioners of alternative medicine, and on topics such as women's health and the politics of health to the general public in adult education classes. She also did a master's degree in psychotherapy and counselling, and worked as a therapist at the Hammersmith Hospital, thinking her days as a medic were finally over.

However, in the 1990s she was lucky enough to discover the British Society for Ecological Medicine (BSEM), a group of doctors and other practitioners who practise nutritional and environmental medicine. They were asking the same questions that had gone unanswered for her throughout medical school. And they were finding answers, helping their patients to attain dramatically better health through changes in diet and nutrition, and through detoxification.

Jenny trained with the BSEM's post-grad course, and qualified in Ecological Medicine, learning in depth about the nutritional and environmental factors that affect our physical and mental health, and passing this information on to her patients and students. She has been practising Ecological Medicine for 22 years now, with a special interest in fertility, pre-conception care and working with children. She is continually seeing the devastating effects of pollution upon people's health and is excited to be able to use her knowledge of biochemistry to remove these environmental toxins from their bodies, make them better, and teach them how to avoid such contamination in the future.

Having studied the environmental history of hundreds of patients, she is now deeply committed to explaining the bigger picture – that what we are doing on most of our farms and elsewhere on our planet profoundly affects the food we eat, the water we drink and the air we breathe, and therefore affects the health of our bodies and minds. This could be summed up as a transition from Pharma to Farmer (Jenny does have a small allotment).

Jenny is the author of "Staying Alive in Toxic Times: A Seasonal Guide to Lifelong Health", published in January 2020 and she is currently writing another book.

Jenny has two children, and it is thanks to her daughter that I met Jenny twenty-three years ago and we became friends. We have a shared interest in ecological medicine and nutrition, and a love of Nature.

When did you start to connect with Nature?

I started to connect with Nature at a very early age. When I was about three years old, we had a small garden, and my father gave me a tiny patch of it. It was a little square near the house, and I planted daisies, pansies, and French marigolds. I loved that little patch of earth.

My mother used to take me to the park around the corner and we used to feed the ducks on the pond. My strongest memory of that park is a beautiful weeping willow tree. My mother would say, "Let's pretend it's our little house, let's go inside it". We went "inside" the willow tree (under its drooping-to-the-ground branches) and I remember the sense of being within this living being, surrounded by the beauty of the tree. That was very special.

When I was 9 years old, we moved to a smaller house, but with a much bigger garden.

My dad gave me a huge area at the back, where I planted tulips. My interest in gardening was sparked right then and I tended those tulip patches till I left home at 18.

When I was about 7 years old, I joined the Woodcraft Folk, which was an alternative breakaway from the Scouts, part of the co-operative movement. We went camping, built campfires, lived outdoors, and would go for very long hikes and learn the names of all the wildflowers in the hedgerows and all the trees.

I had to walk to primary school from when I was 5 years old, along a busy main road. I found the pollution from the cars and lorries unbearable, even back then in the 1960s, and I promised myself, around the age of 7 or 8, that I was going to live in the countryside when I grew up. Sadly, that's something I still haven't managed.

I think the most powerful moment of connecting with Nature for me happened when I was about 10 years old. My brother, who is 12 years older than me, fell in love with a girl from the Highlands of Scotland. We went to visit her family, who were crofters on the far northwest coast.

I still remember walking into this ancient stone cottage and looking out of the window, seeing just sea and sky, seals and seagulls, and the green mountains behind. It was absolutely beautiful. Sitting on the rocks by the sea gave me a sense of coming home, and it is still my favourite place on the planet. It was very calm, and I would say that was probably my first spiritual experience, sensing the magic of that perfect, unpolluted part of the world. However, it has to be said, it was summer; it is less idyllic up there in the winter, when it's not just cold and wet, but dark most of the time!

I was always aware that something was missing growing up in a concrete London suburb. Someone once told me, "You can't put roots down through concrete" and that is how I felt as a child. In the summer these days I stand barefoot on the grass whenever I can, to feel that direct connection. This is not a New Age hippie thing, it is 'A' level physics, electromagnetic fields. (OK, maybe it's also a hippie thing!)

Did you ever lose the connection and get out of tune with Nature?

No. As a teenager, I joined a Jewish socialist youth group, and we went camping much as I'd done in the Woodcraft Folk. We would go on more adventurous hikes: all-night hikes, canoeing on the river Wye on the Welsh border and so on. We learned skills like building a fire, pitching a tent, etc. and it all just deepened my love of Nature.

I would say I never lost the connection in terms of a longing; I only lost it in the sense that there were weeks or months when I couldn't get out of the city, but I never stopped yearning for it. And now that I'm old and retired, it's easier, going away for a weekend or just going for a walk in the woods and fields from our front door. I do that every single day because it's absolutely essential for physical maintenance as well as spiritual sustenance.

What effects does the connection with Nature have on your life?

For me, the connection with Nature has always been a necessity, but there is also an analytic, intellectual side to it: When I wrote my first book "Staying Alive in Toxic Times: A Seasonal Guide to Lifelong Health", I was focused on the nutritional medicine that I've been doing for 23 years. If your food is disconnected from Nature, it's bad for your body, because your body is part of the earth. If you're eating processed food that is such a long way from a plant that it might as well be totally manufactured in a factory, then you're not nourishing yourself on any level.

So, I started looking into what we're doing to the earth: what intensive farming is doing to the soil, how it drains out the nutrients, and how it puts in the pesticides and all the toxic fertilisers that go straight from the soil to your plate to your gut, to your bloodstream, to your brain. Over-farming, which has been happening since the end of the Second World War, drains too many nutrients out of the soil, so we end up eating food that is devoid of the nourishment we need. And if pesticides are being used, which they are if it's not organic farming, we are eating the pesticides and they're damaging our body, particularly the brain.

Through studying with the British Society of Ecological Medicine (BSEM), I have learned how connected this industrial farming is with our current epidemics of cancer, diabetes, heart disease, dementia, and autoimmune diseases like MS. The psycho-spiritual bedrock was already there for me, because I always knew on a deep intuitive level that we cannot be disconnected from Nature. Nature is simply the everything in which we are embedded; we are absolutely, inextricably part of Nature.

As a nutritional/environmental doctor for 23 years, helping people get better by reconnecting with Nature in the form of eating natural foods, living more in tune with the seasons and starting to avoid and detox industrial pollutants from their systems - that is just QED; it's a "no-brainer". Sometimes I'd get people to sprout seedlings on the window ledge, so they've got instant home-grown salad; everyone can do this; everyone has got a window ledge. We have an allotment now, and to eat a cabbage or a potato that we've grown in our own little patch feels very special; it reawakens the sense of connection.

Noticing the toxins in our environment is partly a result of my connection with Nature, as well as my education from the BSEM. I'm in the process of writing a second book, about the ways in which whatever we do to the Earth, we do to our bodies, we do to ourselves. The book will include explanations of environmental toxins such as plastics, fluoride, chlorine, heavy metals, air pollution, car fumes and all the sprays and potions that we use in our homes: how they are making us ill, and how surprisingly easy it is to avoid most of them.

Why do you think modern society has lost its connection with Nature?

Modern society started losing its connection with Nature about 200 or 300 years ago, with the Industrial Revolution. But you could also say that process has been going on for the last 10,000 years. Because until 10,000 years ago, which is incredibly recent in terms of our biological evolution, we were hunter gatherers and lived in the forest. Then, for reasons we still do not fully understand, some hunter gatherers stopped hunting and gathering, and began domesticating plants and animals. They started settling down to become agriculturalists or pastoralists, rather than catching wild animals and picking wild plants.

People didn't have to go so far if they planted seeds on their doorstep, so they stopped being nomadic. Perhaps this was the beginning of "the tyranny of convenience". But once you have a system of settled farming, you have ownership. And once there is ownership, there is war and the accumulation of power, cities and specialisation developing. Everyone in a hunter gatherer tribe could do virtually everything, they all knew how to survive. Once there was agriculture there was surplus, so not everyone had to farm and some people could develop new skills; do pottery, become healers, etc. etc. Of course, there is a plus side to that, because if we were all still hunter gatherers now, we wouldn't have Mozart or Shakespeare. But the downside is war, violence, accumulation of power, and ownership in a way that simply isn't possible in a nomadic, hunter gatherer lifestyle.

As mentioned before, the Industrial Revolution had a big part to play in the disconnection with Nature.

It was gradually happening from the end of the Middle Ages onwards, but it really took off in the early 19th century, when suddenly people were taken off the land where they had been living for many centuries, forced by economic pressures to migrate to the big cities, particularly Manchester, Birmingham and London, and work in factories. It broke up the family, because the family had been the unit of production and there wasn't a work-home divide as we have today. Everybody had worked at home/on the farm. The Industrial Revolution obliterated all that; women had to go to work in factories, children were sent down the mines or to the mills. It was brutal, and it was also very toxic chemically. Young boys were sent up chimneys and ended up with testicular cancer from the poisonous soot in the chimneys. If you read Dickens, you get a good picture of what all this did to people's bodies and souls. And suddenly, no more vitamin D from sunlight. People no longer worked outdoors, and anyway the sunlight couldn't get through the polluted air of our major cities in the UK, with many cases of rickets as a result.

The food was no longer grown, fresh and locally, in your own backyard, and that is when food adulteration began, in the 19th century. The "food manufacturing" industry became a thing, and we know now that food which is manufactured is not real food. You pick an apple, you catch a fish, you grow a cabbage: that is food. Something that comes out of a factory may be just about edible – people can get used to any old junk - but it is not real food.

So, we have messed up big time, and of course this began in Britain, but we exported industry and all its pollutants to the rest of the world. The population has exploded and that's partly because there's nothing to slow it down. If you go back to hunter gatherer tribes, even those living today like the Hadza people of Tanzania or the Yanomami of the Amazon rainforest, you will see that they space their children naturally; they have a 5–7-year gap between their kids. That's because although they are healthy, they live on the edge of hunger, so that when a woman is breastfeeding, her ovulation stops. (If you are a well-fed Western woman, breastfeeding doesn't reliably prevent conception). Hunter gatherers, being nomadic, couldn't manage a baby if they still had a toddler in tow, because a woman going gathering simply couldn't carry two children. So they had to wait till child number one was independently mobile and could keep up, before having child number two.

Once there was agriculture and a surplus of food, you could have more children, but then you would also have epidemics of infectious diseases, which didn't tend to happen to hunter gatherers, because the bugs couldn't keep up with them as they were always on the move.

If you have a large number of people gathered in one place, you're going to get infectious disease, and so a lot of children died and people kept having more to make up the deficit. Also, if you're a farmer, you want to have lots of kids because they can help you on the farm. If you're a hunter gatherer, you don't want too many mouths to feed. So, the Industrial Revolution made the population explosion worse. And again, many children died.

We have made a mess, and we must clear it up. The connection with Nature, for the vast majority of people, seems to have been terminally lost with the Industrial Revolution, when people's lives were no longer regulated by the cycles of the year, by light and dark. Harvesting in August and September, hunkering down and burning the wood that you chopped previously around the winter solstice, planting seeds in the spring, partying outdoors in the summer; that whole rhythm almost disappeared with the Industrial Revolution. Instead, we had the beginning of the nine to five, the factory bell ringing, getting up when it's still pitch-dark and going to work down the mine or in the factory or office. The Covid pandemic partly put a stop to that routine for some people, but only for the middle classes.

So, we've lost touch with our daily rhythms. Many people work set hours which do not change from winter to summer. An early morning shift is fine in June, but if you must do that in December, it's going to make you ill because you're going against Nature.

Nature tells us to hunker down and hibernate in winter and we shouldn't really be going anywhere, apart from a brisk walk during the daylight hours to tell the brain there is still some daylight out there. Once it gets dark, we shouldn't be using quite so much electricity to keep it light, because it is not real daylight. It should be candlelight or the light of a fire, which is reddish orange like infrared. That glow is calming and gets you ready for sleep.

Children exposing themselves to the white and blue light of their phones are sending the pineal gland in their brain the message that there is a blue sky, and it is morning, so time to wake up, while they should have been asleep for hours.

We have lost the rhythms of day and night, we have lost the rhythm of summer and winter, and all that is incredibly bad for our brains and bodies, but we can regain it fairly simply, by going for a walk in the park.

Our bodies and psyches have not and cannot evolve fast enough to keep up with the extraordinary changes we've created in our environment. And this affects children/teens particularly because we are still tribal by Nature. Nowadays, children can't run outside to play in the fields, because it's not a field or forest outside the door, it is a street with cars going up and down it. Hence the nuclear family has become much more of the environment in which we live, rather than the tribe and the extended family. That's particularly damaging for children.

Then, the minute children are 5 years old or even earlier, we send them to school, where instead of being in a natural, multi-generational community, they're shut in a classroom with a whole bunch of kids who are exactly the same age. So, they don't learn to nurture the younger ones and don't experience how to learn from the older ones. Our education system is reinforcing the disconnection from Nature. But more and more schools are getting gardens now and children are learning how to grow plants, which is great. They should be teaching the kids gardening and cooking. They are more basic subjects than maths!

I honestly think, certainly up until they are teenagers, the kids should be spending 5 or 6 hours doing outdoor sports and gardening, and just 1 or 2 hours doing academic subjects like reading and writing. They will learn just as much academic stuff in those 1 or 2 hours as they would in a long school day, because they will be concentrating and won't be restless, having already met the need to do something physical. Their bodies and brains will function better. I saw this work for real when I home educated my son in the early 2000s; he and all his home-ed friends were so much happier and more relaxed than their mates who were forced to go to school. And they learned faster.

In your opinion, what is the best way for people to get in tune with Nature?

To get in tune with Nature people don't have to move to the countryside; there are birds and trees and flowers in our city parks. It's about taking a moment to stop and stare; to notice. Maybe if you can't connect in a deep emotional/psychological way with Nature, it will be harder for you to tune in to the real urgency of our current ecological crisis. If you've got a cat, maybe you're more able to care about the tigers. If you've got a little plant on your windowsill, that's a microcosm of what is being destroyed globally. We do need that personal connection. I think there are very few people who can't feel it when they get the opportunity. Even just growing a few seeds in a tray or putting a bulb in a pot and seeing the daffodil coming up; very few people are immune to the joy of that.

There are so many changes we can make in our own lives that will make us healthier.

For example, we need to realise how many products we're buying, as well as petrol and diesel, that are actually petrochemical in origin. Every time you put cream from the GP on your child's eczema, it contains steroids, but it also has a petrochemical base. Instead, you could use chickweed, calendula, liquorice, chamomile, burdock and other herbal remedies. If we change to natural medicines, natural cleaning products, natural everything, we're simultaneously saving our own bodies and boycotting the petrochemical industry which is damaging our planet.

If we choose to stop buying air fresheners and toxic petrochemical perfumes, hideous detergents, and the wrong kind of washing up liquid, and if we start buying natural versions of all these products, herbal versions of all our so-called personal care products, if we throw away the toxic deodorant, stop wrapping our food in plastic, and if we stop spraying unnecessary cleaning products around our house, we'll be doing two things: we will no longer be supporting the petrochemical industry that ruins the earth while making these products, and we will be improving our own health.

There are so many safe, natural alternatives! Suma make safe soap and washing up liquid, Ecover make safer laundry products, sodium bicarb is a safe cleaning product for kitchen surfaces, Green People make safe (non-fluoride) toothpaste, Sukin and Weleda do safe moisturisers, and organic essential oils like geranium, lavender, lemongrass, and jasmine can replace your synthetic perfume. I could go on . . .

Getting in tune with Nature is not just about going out for a walk, it is also about pressurising the government to do something about air pollution, because air pollution from car fumes is contributing not only to lung cancer, not only to very dangerous levels of childhood asthma, but also to heart disease, dementia and even diabetes. There are some good organisations working on this, in particular 'Mums for Lungs', The Clean Air Fund and Client Earth. We need to join these pressure groups and we need to walk or cycle wherever we possibly can. Take the side streets, not the main roads, so you don't poison yourself in the effort not to poison others!

Lastly, planting trees is a wonderful way to connect with Nature. If you can't physically plant trees yourself, then you can support one of the wonderful organisations who plant trees in Britain: two of the best are The Woodland Trust and Trees for Life. Happy reconnecting!

❦ Meet Jim – Nature lover, medical director and retired family physician from the USA

Jim Winslow practiced for almost 35 years as a generalist family physician in clinic, hospital, nursing home and emergency department settings in Tarboro, a small town in eastern North Carolina, USA. He has retired twice unsuccessfully and for the past 8 years Jim has worked as medical director and clinician at the local health department, which is within walking distance of his home. Most of what he does now is family planning, sexually transmitted infections, cancer screening, modifying and approving a lot of policies and procedures. He works from eight to five, three days a week, leaving him time for other activities and being out in Nature.

When did you start to connect with Nature?

I think I started to connect with Nature when I was about four or five years old. I remember once, the wind was blowing as I climbed a tree in the backyard. It was an exciting experience being blown back and forth as the treetop swayed in the wind. My brother and my friend from 3 houses down wouldn't climb up, not wanting to get blown around or have the limb break off, I guess. I remember a feeling of connection with something outside myself. It is still a vivid memory.

    I remember at about the same age connecting with Nature by walking barefoot through the clover in the front yard in the summertime and getting stung between the toes by honeybees, a seemingly unavoidable experience at least once every summer. I was scared of honeybees until adulthood. It's only in the last 10 or 15 years that I've gotten friendly with them.

    Another memory from the same age, and the reason I can date this is because when I started kindergarten, we moved to a different home in a different neighborhood. A neighbour, an older lady, would regularly take yesterday's stale biscuits, crumble them beneath a Camelia bush in her backyard, and the birds would fly in to dine on the biscuits. I always got a charge out of that. Seems like there were usually cardinals, red birds to me then. My grandmother had a bird feeder, under a tree outside her dining room. She started me as a birdwatcher. She seemed to have a close relationship with Nature. She could walk up to a beehive and not be afraid or stung. The birds would fly up close when she would fill her bird feeder. I always got excited about that.

I was raised in Tarboro which has about 10,000 residents, but in addition to life in town, I also spent a significant amount of time in rural environments. My grandfather opened a business selling horses and mules in Tarboro in 1905. As he became more prosperous, he acquired land, began farming and ran a dairy. Somewhat involuntarily my father was drawn into the family business. I spent many hours around mules, cattle, woods, and farms as a child.

I've been an enthusiastic camper and hiker since childhood and an enthusiastic backpacker since my teenage years. I've logged hundreds of miles backpacking in the eastern and western US, especially along the Appalachian Trail, which runs from Georgia in the southern United States to Maine in the extreme northern United States, along the crest of the Appalachian Mountain chain. Early on I would go with friends and family, sometimes with teenage children, if we were lucky. Over time friends and family became less available and I ended up going out solo. What a satisfying physical and spiritual experience it is to be immersed in the sights and sounds, even smells, and rhythms of Nature.

Did you ever lose the connection and get out of tune with Nature?

I wouldn't say that I lost the connection with Nature, but there were periods when it seemed less accessible, especially during the time when I was being trained and educated. However, when I was taking tenth grade (age 16) biology, I well remember one afternoon in the laboratory as I was looking through a microscope at some tiny aquatic creatures and algae, hearing a voice in my head say, "Winslow, you're home, you're going to be a biologist one day". So, studying biology in college, even though it was largely molecular biology, I still felt there was a connection with Nature, because in a pretty basic way, I was learning how Nature worked, which maybe, arguably, made my connection with Nature closer, even though I wasn't spending much time in Nature. When I was able, I still had a longing for natural experiences. My wife Kathy and I kept a bird feeder in the backyard during my residency training and participated occasionally in birding trips with the local Audubon Society. In 1977 Kathy, my brother and I took three weeks off, to travel around Ireland by bicycle. We spent lots of time grooving on Nature, sights, getting in the zone, and drinking Guinness of course! I consciously used that trip to Ireland to be able to be outdoors and do something different, as a reward for myself.

Even though I couldn't be in Nature as much in the 70's, I was able to make myself promises of Nature. Florida was a great place for birdwatching. I have come to find birding a very important natural experience for me. While birding whether at home or in the field, whether sitting, standing, walking, I feel alert to whatever is around me and delightfully, soothingly, refreshingly present. I think that's part of Nature's attraction for me, just being present.

What effect(s) does your connection with Nature have on your life?

My connection with Nature has given me calmness and peace of mind. I have felt love from Nature; I feel love for Nature. I think Nature loves us and provides for us. We can love Nature back and nurture it. It seems like a process of coevolution. I feel a sense of closeness, a sense of partnership with Nature because of that. When I spend time in Nature, it's like I'm immersed in a slowly flowing river. I like feeling the connection when I'm not being stung by the bees.

Nature has spoken to me and given me advice. Several years ago, I was having stressful ruminations about retirement. One evening I went outside for some fresh air and some star time. I found the Big Dipper, the North Star, Cassiopeia, Orion. I wanted to find Sirius, the Dog Star; I had never identified it before. I found a bright star close to Orion, and I thought,

"Are you the Dog Star, are you Sirius? As I stood there, I felt the Dog Star twinkle back at me and say "Yes, Jim, I'm the Dog Star and I'm as 'serious' as I can be. Look, I've been up here doing this a long time, Jim, and you, look at you, you're taking things way too seriously. Now take a lesson and chill out". A few weeks after my tongue in cheek admonishment by the Dog Star, I heard by an improbable sequence of events that they needed help at the health department. On a whim I went back to work with a light heart. It seems to have suited me. Seems unreal now.

I think that Nature is bigger than we realise. I joined the International Society for the Study of Subtle Energies and Energy Medicine in the 90's. They explored the idea that there are subtle energies at play in the world which probably have a scientific basis, but we haven't been able to measure them. They study things like therapeutic touch, distance healing, psychoneuroimmunology, meditation, Reiki, Qi Gong, aura manipulation, placebo, and other energetic healings. I thought it would be interesting to learn more about energies from a scientific point of view and to be in contact with the people who are practicing those things. Being a healing practitioner of Western medicine myself, I knew there was more to healing than the evidence-based practice that I was taught.

Two of my natural refuges have been keeping a backyard eco-jungle-garden and riding my bicycle on quiet rural roads. Tarboro is small enough that I don't have to go somewhere else to ride my bicycle. I can just hop on it, and within a mile or so I'm beyond the city limits. Over the past several years I have encountered and often rescued every species of turtle we have in the area and many other herps. I've learned from their voices where the chorus frogs, the spring peepers and the squirrel treefrogs live.

Why do you think modern society has lost its connection with Nature?

I don't have any earth-shaking ideas, but I think that much of modern society has migrated away from Nature. With populations concentrating in urban areas, people are finding fewer opportunities to be in touch with Nature. I have read that the stars are not visible at night in too many places because of the ambient light. Getting to Nature is harder than it used to be for many of us.

We have these attractive, easily accessible electronic experiences that may or may not be as fulfilling as natural experiences, but they are always available with the tap of a finger.

I suspect that some of us find the prospect of contact with Nature daunting, given widespread publicity regarding threats to personal safety. Seems like a widespread cinematic theme for decades has been that you're not safe anywhere. Remember *Invasion of the Body Snatchers*, *Terminator*, *The Matrix*. I believe that theme has loomed larger in our lives in recent years.

I wonder whether we may harbour some feelings of guilt over our treatment of Nature over time and avoid it for that reason.

I think we've lost some of our connection with Nature through our diets, which have become more divorced from Nature over time. Don't you feel more connected to Nature, when you're eating a banana, a tomato, a peanut, a fish, sushi? What is it they say, "If it wouldn't look like food to your grandmother, then don't eat it"?

In your opinion, what is the best way for people to get in tune with Nature?

Go outside and look up into the sky regularly. It's remarkable the Nature that goes on overhead morning, afternoon, and night. If you like what you see, you'll probably get hooked on the experience. If you don't like what you see, then what can you change?

Plant a garden. Keep earthworms. Keep a compost pile. Join a Community Sponsored Agriculture (CSA) group. That can put you in touch with local Nature, including the soil and the weather. I have a 16 x16 foot garden in the backyard. One year I planted a fall cover crop of buckwheat. The following spring, when the buckwheat began to bloom, the garden was alive with flying, buzzing insects visiting the blossoms, native bees, wasps, flies, butterflies. It was such a celebration of life that I couldn't bring myself to turn the buckwheat under to plant my spring garden. Earthworms love melon rind. The local peanuts that you roast yourself are much superior to the packaged variety in my experience.

Bring Nature indoors. Every year I look forward to late December. In the Human Services building where I work, the health department clinics are on the sixth floor. In December sunsets occur near the usual end of the workday. The breakroom has a west facing window shielded from the north by a perpendicular outside wall. The room opens onto a 90-foot hallway. Only in late December, around the time of the winter solstice, does the sun set in a southerly enough position for the setting sun to shine through the window, the doorway and down the long hallway, throwing light on the wall at the far end of it. Each year I feel in tune with my solar system and connected with my stone age forebears at Newgrange or Stonehenge.

Exercise outdoors. I give my patients exercise prescriptions. The beneficial effects of outdoor exercise in a natural setting are well established. I think that to be in tune with Nature, to connect with Nature is to feel yourself part of Nature. Bike rides can do that for me. To feel the wind blowing, the joy of a tailwind, the hurt with a headwind, to see rural vistas, the tall pine trees, the towering cypresses, the turtles on a log at the river or creek bank, the birds soaring, perching, hopping around, to hear the woodpeckers piping or shrieking in the woods, a kingfisher cackling, the plant life signalling the changing of the seasons, the frog voices signalling the changing of the seasons, the bird species that are present signalling the changing of the seasons, those put me in tune with Nature.

Start early introducing children to Nature and I'll bet the attunement will stick. There is a local African-American church here that has received national awards for a program introduced by its energetic pastor to get outdoors, exercise, plant and tend garden plots, sell produce through a CSA arrangement, distribute fresh vegetables to those in need, keep beehives and sell honey. Imagine the likely enduring connection to Nature and the mental, physical, spiritual benefits for the community. The Appalachian Trail Conservancy has a concerted program to get youth out into Nature.

🌿 Meet Joe – Entrepreneur and former pro swimmer

Joe is a former professional swimmer turned entrepreneur. He competed for Scotland at the 2014 Commonwealth Games, after training 25 hours per week for several years.

He likes to connect dots, make things happen, and get people to smile more.

Joe was born in Scotland but moved to the South of France when he was a year old. The family lived in a very rural area, and Joe spent a lot of time outdoors.

Joe built and sold Motion Nutrition, a supplement company. This is how I met him. Being a nutritional therapist, I regularly used his supplements, personally and in practice.

Joe is now Managing Director of Knowjack Media, a photo, video, and events production agency for outdoor-led brands.

He always struck me as a very outdoorsy person, who wouldn't contemplate the idea of not living an active, outdoor life. His enthusiasm is infectious, and I was wondering if he would be as enthusiastic about Nature as he is about wellness, entrepreneurship, and sport.

Here is his story.

When did you start to connect with Nature?

I grew up in a very remote part of Southern France, surrounded by forest. We would walk out of the house, which was an old stone barn, straight into the woods.

My earliest memories are of building makeshift tree houses, climbing the neighbour's big lime tree and jumping into the nearby lake. To me it just felt normal to have my hands in the dirt, climb trees or cycle in the woods. It was almost more normal to be outside than inside. It was where I felt most at 'home', being outdoors. There was no real effort to connect with Nature, nor was an introduction to Nature from my parents necessary, it was just normal. Unlike many people, who experience a separation between regular life and Nature, I've always been connected to Nature.

My connection with Nature was a physical one, but in a way, also emotional, as from quite a young age, I was able to be free outside. By the time I was 7 years old, I would cycle about two miles to my school in the morning and then cycle back in the afternoon. That is something that is hard to imagine now. I think it's partly because this was pre-internet and before the excess worrying about the state of the world. I don't think things have changed that much. I think people just worry more now. The area where we used to live is still incredibly remote and rural. I don't think there has been any more crime in 2022 than there was in 1997. It's just that we worry a lot more.

As a child I certainly took Nature for granted, but I also sometimes felt overwhelmed by the vastness of Nature. Sometimes I felt like it was a lot of work to get anywhere far, or I felt quite small.

When I was a teenager, I got frustrated sometimes because I had to rely on my parents to get to town. I would have wanted to spend more time in town and be able to see people more easily, but I still don't think I would have wanted to change anything and live in town.

I was happy to be in our 'wild area'.

I had a dirt bike and liked going into the woods, a different type of fun from when I was a child.

The connection with Nature was kept all along, even when I moved back to the UK and started university in Scotland. Stirling is quite a small town, and it is surrounded by beautiful landscapes. So, I felt like I was still in Nature there. It was very easy to go out for hikes, etc.

Did you ever lose the connection and get out of tune with Nature?

Living in London during the pandemic was difficult. Confining myself to a small apartment, with limited time outdoors, felt alien and extremely uncomfortable. Moving to London was not a problem as there are so many parks. It was about being in an apartment. Like an ant trapped inside the mound. It also prompted a move to the south coast for easier access to sea and land.

How did you reconnect?

My wife and I moved to the south coast of England. From here, we can walk to the bottom of the street and jump into the sea, we have a beautiful park just next door, and we can access the South Downs within 15 minutes. Despite being in a densely populated region, it feels freeing to have so many options for quickly and easily accessing Nature.

Work changed my connection with Nature too. About two years ago I co-founded Knowjack Media, a photo, video, and events production agency for outdoor-led brands. It's all about getting people outdoors. And it is great, as we not only get to work with cool brands, but we also get to work outdoors.

What effects does the connection with Nature have on your life?

Here's how I see it: it's difficult to be angry at the world when you've started off your day in Nature. Whether that is a bike ride along the coast, a quick dip in the sea, or a walk in the woods; this connection makes me feel lighter and happier. It gives perspective to whatever is going on in my life.

The connection with Nature is so energising. I think that people tend to think that in the UK you don't get enough sunshine or that the sunshine is not strong enough. And that's partially true. In my view, the biggest problem is that people just don't get outdoors anywhere near enough. And we think that you can just take vitamin D and forget about going outside. But that's not how the human body works. It is energising when you get pure sunshine and daylight on your skin. And then of course we are also a little bit obsessed with protecting our eyes and skin against sunlight here. If we do go out it's with factor 50 sunscreen and sunglasses. You might as well stay indoors then.

If I'm going through periods where, for whatever reason, I'm not able to get outside enough, I definitely feel less energised, and my sleep quality will start to decrease quite a bit. So those are all physical benefits of being connected to Nature. It is so obvious.

Sometimes you can't be bothered to go out for a walk or go into the sea. But when you do 20 minutes of that, you will notice how much better you feel immediately afterwards.

Why do you think modern society has lost its connection with Nature?

It's easy to get lost in a mix of digital and concrete jungles. There is always something new to learn, watch, complete or answer. Today, it's impossible to finish our to-do lists. It's like a web page with an infinity-scroll: you never reach the bottom. Yet, it's also hard to know when to stop, look up, and step outside. The gravitational pull from our mobile phones makes it difficult to switch off and immerse ourselves in Nature. It's a habit we all need to work on, as the science is clear: time outdoors makes us feel better.

I am still hopeful though that, in the long term, this disconnection will change.

All the benefits are so obvious that you can't ignore them. I feel there needs to be a big change. If you look at it from a generational point of view, I don't feel anywhere near as optimistic. If you were either born with a smartphone in your hand, or you were still a teenager or in your early twenties when you got one, you are in trouble as nobody knew how addictive smart phones would be. The older generation never got that same addiction.

I would hope, for the younger generation whose parents have experienced what smartphones can do to us, that they will be a bit more mindful about it.

I think a lot of people are totally submerged in entertainment. Not so much entertainment, like watching movies, but stimulation. I know many people who don't spend a second of their waking hours not being stimulated by something. Listening to music or podcasts through their earphones, looking at the small screen on their phones, looking at the big screens for work, big TV screens in the evening, etc. If you have grown up like that and nobody has made you aware of how bad it is, it's hard to realise.

In your opinion, what is the best way for people to get in tune with Nature?

Not everyone is going to adore hiking. But each of us can find something we love doing outdoors. Finding something you enjoy is the only way to create a life-long habit.

Our son is starting nursery when he is 2 years old, and we have found a lovely place where the children spend a lot of time outdoors. We would like him to be immersed in Nature, so it is part of his life.

🌿 Meet Lou – Naturopath, Adventurer and Skydiver

Raised in the Australian outdoors with an abundance of family and community, it was only natural that these would develop into core values within Louise. She went on to study naturopathy in the late nineties and with a backpack and an adventurous spirit set off and travelled the world extensively, gained international experience in the worlds of naturopathy, integrative health, product, brand, and business development (with a dash of skydiving here and there too) - all with a continued love of the natural world, community, and curiosity.

I hardly know anyone who loves life as much as Lou does, she is a force of Nature, always on the go and always living life to the full. Her story is not only full of connection with Nature, human connection is also an extremely important part.

When did you start to connect with Nature?

Thankfully I didn't need to make a conscious choice in this. My wonderful family are responsible for constant, effortless exposure to what is in my opinion some of the most wonderous natural environments around.

We are from a small coastal part of Australia, in a unique climate where the mountain range is close to the ocean, enabling us to have a diverse landscape from rainforest, farmed land, crystal clear rivers to empty long white beaches. The two rivers that run through our homeland meet the ocean, creating breath-taking scenery, but it's so much more than that. It is how we interacted with all this and how this connection became intertwined in our lifestyle that is so important.

Urunga is on Gumbaynggirr land, and my heart and soul belong there.

Where the rivers meet the sea is a wooden boardwalk, that hovers just about the sand flats, alongside the mangroves and out along the river mouth to the ocean and beach off to the side. It's part of the community, it's a place where you can either be alone or catch up with your family, friends and of course the local gossip. when I'm back home I ride my bike most mornings, and with a thermos of tea I walk out to watch the sunrise. Rarely a brief trip, as the social scene is always abundant and more so if you are a local, but the bathing in sea air and the views all around hold for me therapy of the most powerful kind.

One of my earliest memories is something my family used to call the mandarin raid. Imagine it's the early 80's and a few rattly old double decker buses are collecting anyone who is willing to travel from town out to our old farm to pick as many mandarins as they could carry, picnic along the banks of the Never Never River and if you were willing to brave the cold water, go for a swim too.

This is just one example of how we as a family came together in Nature. This must have modelled my character more than I can summarise, as I have always been that person who makes the table longer, notices the person in the corner and says, "Hey, wanna join?" Community and connection form part of my personality and core values.

My father is a keen fisherperson, and this is still something we enjoy doing together, whenever possible. It was these endless fishing adventures that held many lessons about the value of mangroves, corals, best places to collect seaweed, animal lifecycles, only taking what you need and leaving it better than when you arrived (something I wish I could say hand on heart was always achieved) and how to share what you have, when you land back with your neighbours. The sentiments always returned, veggies left on your doorstep without note or expectation of thanks.

Camping was our way of holidaying. We were not a wealthy family and, holy heck, am I forever grateful for that. For years we had what felt like an annual pilgrimage out to an island in the Great Barrier Reef called Lady Musgrave. My dad would volunteer as the park ranger and we would camp, after having been dropped off by a boat, with our water and supplies, and left to be self-sufficient for weeks, in total immersion of reef life and deep exposure to Nature.

There is such power in the rhythm your body takes when there is only Nature to direct its pulse. The peace of sunrises, the background beat of waves, cicadas, bird chorus and sometimes the piercing scream of Nature getting too close to someone.

With the natural curiosity that comes with youth, we had an endless amount of stimulation from the natural world to keep our minds educated and challenged always.

The wealth of my childhood experiences is not lost on me, and I will be forever grateful to my parents, siblings, and community.

You are probably wondering where the naturopathy came in. Well, when I was about 15 years old, I had to do work experience at high school. I found it difficult to choose what to do, as I didn't want just to slot into a career. I can remember the careers advisor sitting down with me and we had a very open exploratory conversation about what really interested me, etc. I was used to being outdoors and was also growing up in an alternative community. Where I went to high school was very much the hippie epicentre of the East coast of Australia. I was probably quite exposed to challenging the norm. I was always thinking about different approaches. And the more the career advisor spoke to me, the more I realised that I was already going to the health food shop and seeking therapies myself. It turned out that there was a Naturopathy College about 20 minutes from my house. So, at 15 years old, I did my workplace experience at that naturopathic college, and I got to sit in on lots of courses, but I also got to observe clinical consultations. I saw how they were approaching healthcare, tailoring herbal remedies for each person plus the value of lifestyle therapies like massage. It was what I was always looking for in terms of a personalised system.

Whilst studying I was working in pharmacy; this was great exposure to allopathic medicine and the space where both can peacefully coexist. I graduated when I was 21 years old, and I realise now how young I was! But I went straight into clinical practice. First at a homeopathic clinic, then at an aesthetics naturopathy clinic, before setting up within several chiropractic clinics.

Did you ever lose the connection and get out of tune with Nature?

After years of back packing, a bit of an Aussie cliché, I landed back in the UK with the plan of staying for a few years. It was coming into autumn and soon winter. I had not really lived in winter like this before. Living in

London I soon found my shoulders hunched and my knowledge of living in a cooler climate was inadequate. My life became more indoors than ever.

I have to say, I recently felt the disconnection again too. Having founded part of a company, building/investing in teams, vision, products, and navigating through the joys of 2020-2022 and more. I was longing for re-immersion into the pace of Nature. My standing desk is lovely, the people incredible, but it has not been the best of platforms for how I engage with Nature.

What caused this disconnection?

You could say the disconnection with Nature was caused by location, but it was of course more than that. It was learning a new environment, being foreign from the trees, not truly having lived through seasons. And heck, not understanding how to layer, what makes a good winter coat, that the outdoors might not always be inviting from a tropical perspective but that there are also gifts hidden within that. The leaves even check out for a while.

How did you reconnect?

This may be a little extreme for some people but it's my story. I always wanted to skydive. It was how high and vast the sky in Australia felt, and on the occasions, we drove near a skydiving place, my neck would swing around in the car, making sure I watched every second of the sight.

I did my first tandem when I turned sixteen and topped up with another from time to time. So, when I finally qualified to skydive that was it, it was motivation to re-embrace the outdoors. I needed to get that layering sorted out, not only for the ground temperatures, but for the temperatures at 15,000 feet in all seasons!

With a new outdoor hobby and tribe, I was back camping every weekend, surrounded by an instant family from all backgrounds. I was waking up to the morning chorus soundtrack of the UK and being exposed to the many seasons that happened each day. There is no warm escape on an open airfield when you are waiting around for the rain/clouds/wind/hail to clear. The people made it worthwhile, and the skydiving soon became more natural to me.

What effects does the connection with Nature have on your life?

For me, the connection with Nature is softening. I am what people would call an extrovert, but really, I am an ambivert. I feed off the energy around me, but equally, I need that calming time - the time that others do not need to witness. When I am in Nature and truly connected with it, I soften. My activity calms, my energy is more balanced, and my breath is paced evenly. This softening welcomes an awakened awareness, and from here the creative self sparkles.

Why do you think modern society has lost its connection with Nature?

There seems to be an obsession with occupation, a busyness and competition in ourselves and maybe conscious or not, with others. This occupation, coming in the form of things, our desires for more, our disconnection within technology and the numbing it can provide to a wired and frazzled nervous system. It stops the softening that helps us to be vulnerable and open to different kinds of opportunities.

Modernity, for generations, idealised progression in forms of urbanisation, but thankfully there is a turning point in motion for some of this. We are welcoming Nature back into these spaces. Aware that displaced Nature in turn displaces us too.

In your opinion, what is the best way for people to get in tune with Nature?

There is no gold standard and I avoid the idealisation of Nature bathing that media projects. Just like self-care is not just a facemask or a bath bomb, connecting with Nature doesn't have to mean climbing a pristine landscape or travelling to the most exotic of places. It can be cloud watching, observing your environment, leaving your phone in your pocket, and seeing how many deer you can spot out of the train window. Sure, I crave being back in my homeland and feeling the sand and water on my skin, how the sun and salt nurture me in ways too powerful to be replaced by a product.

We have got this perfectionist view of what chasing Nature is, but we can just stop and look at the beautiful plant in front of us. It doesn't have to be so idyllic. I think the world we live in can be very much an office urban environment, where we bring the natural elements in.

We can modify our environment quite quickly.

Getting in tune with Nature is simply allowing it space in your life, and once this is done it will take the next steps for you.

❧ Meet Mariel & Gerbrand – Owners and Guardians of the 'Mengelmoestuin' in the Netherlands

Mariel and her partner Gerbrand are the owners and guardians of the 'Mengelmoestuin' (meaning the Medley Garden in English), an organic, biodynamic garden in Ammerstol, the Netherlands.

They have always been looking for a more conscious, balanced, and relaxed lifestyle, and this is how the idea was born to try and be as self-sufficient as possible and live off their garden.

In 2000 Mariel and Gerbrand sold their house and belongings to travel wherever the wind would take them, nothing was pre-planned. They travelled to the Middle East, Asia, and Bali. After 2½ years of travelling, they arrived home with the idea that they should be doing whatever is closest to their heart, preferably together, and in close harmony with the cosmos.

They created a garden on a piece of wasteland until Mariel became ill and had to be treated for cancer. Being outdoors and working in Nature had a healing effect on her, so by the end of 2006 they decided to buy a plot of land and continue their 'Mengelmoestuin' garden.

Mariel had done various herb workshops and she embarked on an herbal medicine course. She loves working with the native herbs that grow in the direct environment. After all, what people need always grows near them. That is how Nature works. Gerbrand retrained as a horticulturist.

Their garden is first and foremost meant to feed them, allowing them to be self-sufficient, but they also like to share with others. They are regularly selling produce, but as the 'Mengelmoestuin' is a non-profit, private garden, the income is all invested back into the project.

Mariel kindly agreed to collaborate by sharing their story.

When did you start to connect with Nature?

I think I started to connect with Nature at a very young age. I was always playing outdoors and wasn't averse to mud and pig muck. I didn't build dens, but I dug holes that I could crawl into. I didn't inherit my love for Nature from my parents. It skipped a generation. My grandmother was a keen gardener who used to pick rose hips in the park, for instance, and canned and preserved her harvest. Her sister was a bulb farmer in Northern Holland, who also had a magnificent kitchen garden.

I always felt best being outdoors, in the open air, where I could breathe. That is why we have been living in a yurt for the past 5 years, in close contact with my garden and animals.

In Nature there was a sense of trust, freedom, and peace, but always with a certain respect. I behaved myself like a guest. As a matter of fact, I still do that now. I always experience Nature, be it animals or greenery, as a higher power.

I have always had a physical relationship with Nature. As a child, being outdoors meant playing. But there was also an emotional element. I noticed that especially when I was about 15 years old, I needed to be surrounded by Nature. When I moved to Amsterdam I was 17 years old, and I would regularly go to a park, but I always missed the wideness of the polder.

After a year in the big city, I returned to my roots. I started working on a ferry, with daily exposure to wind and water. I loved it! I lived in a cemetery with high beech trees, owls, and lots of greenery; it was wonderful. And for an extra dose of Nature exposure, I would cycle through the polder.

Did you ever lose the connection and get out of tune with Nature?

I never really lost the connection with Nature, but I do remember working in an office when I was 28 years old. I had no contact with the outdoors, didn't see the sky and didn't know what the weather was like. I only lasted there for three weeks; I didn't realise how quickly I had to leave.

Conversations on the Lost Connection with Nature

How did you reconnect?

I always had a connection with Nature. I walked a lot, while feeling and experiencing Nature I always wanted to be outdoors as much as possible, either to work with trees, plants, and herbs, or just to observe.

What effects does the connection with Nature have on your life?

For the last 25 years I have been moving freely in Nature, with several years in Asia. For 18 years I have worked in our 'Mengelmoestuin' garden now and it is all-important, my whole being is set to it and focused on it. Nature gives, cures, comforts, and heals. I couldn't live without it.

In our garden we work with Nature and not against it, and we are closely following what is happening in the cosmos, as the moon, planets and stars have an impact on how plants grow.

Everything that grows in the garden is edible and/or usable. There are many native trees and shrubs of which the fruits and leaves are being used to produce jams, jellies, herbal teas, and juices. NO green houses or polytunnels are being used, because we think that it is the only way the crops can be one with the cosmos.

Our herb garden is full of medicinal, native herbs, and all through the garden you can find wild herbs growing too. We use some of the herbs to make teas, salves, oils, and tinctures.

Why do you think modern society has lost its connection with Nature?

Imagine living on the third floor in a flat in an urban area, where you are just trying to survive. Working, ordering food, commuting, and hanging out in front of the TV. Hopefully you will go to a park or the woods for a walk on a Sunday afternoon. Often life is all about being as comfortable as possible. And for that you won't need Nature, right?

We don't have a TV, are in bed by 10pm, only have cold water, and we need to chop our wood for the wood burner. Most people start shaking their head when I tell them this.

In your opinion, what is the best way for people to get in tune with Nature?

People getting in tune with Nature? Will they ever succeed in this?

People like their comfort and don't like having to take a step back. A lot of people don't really know what Nature is any more. They still see it as something you need to control. They don't dare walk into the woods without a map, because they imagine you would get lost. Goodness knows what horrible things can happen! So, a lot of natural areas have been made 'family-proof', with playgrounds, boardwalks, information boards, etc.

There are people who move to a rural area, plant loads of trees and then get terribly stressed when wildlife appears. This then becomes a problem that must be solved.

To be honest, I am not very optimistic, it is the way of the world. Maybe I'm seeing it this way because today I have to be indoors, because it is raining and cold. Although days like that can be nice too.

We have several volunteers, who help us in the garden. It is wonderful to experience how these people become more comfortable in their own skin through contact with Nature.

We enjoy giving these people an opportunity to feel better and more relaxed.

🐝 Meet Marion – Beekeeper & Retired Biologist

Marion Cooper is a remarkable woman, who at the age of 85, together with her 88-year-old husband, is still managing about 20 beehives and processing around 500 pounds of honey a year.

Marion wanted to study medicine, but because she failed a physics exam, she had to settle for another science course, so with the background given to her by her naturalist father, she chose biology. She graduated from Royal Holloway, University of London with a degree in Biological Sciences. For 10 years she worked for the Civil Service in a plant pathology lab, specialising in viral diseases, later moving to animal pathology. Although she loved her jobs, she did miss the human contact that she would have had as a doctor.

Her career progressed into scientific, mainly agricultural literature, so there was an obvious connection with Nature there. With a colleague Marion wrote a book called 'Poisonous Plants and Fungi in Britain: Animal and Human Poisoning', followed by another, 'Poisonous Plants and Fungi: An Illustrated Guide'. Both were published by the government Stationery Office.

I met Marion through my husband, who, like her, is a very keen beekeeper. I have always been impressed with her knowledge of plants and her enthusiasm for beekeeping. And I really want to mention here her fabulous baking skills; she often enters biscuits and cakes for the Honey Shows, with particularly good results. This book would not be complete without her.

When did you start to connect with Nature?

From my very earliest recollections as a really small child, my connection with Nature started mainly through my father, who was the son of a dairy and arable farmer. My father was an old-style naturalist and - to me - seemed to know everything about everything in my natural world.

We lived on a nursery, as my father was a market gardener/plantsman by profession, but his interests were far wider than the plants with which he worked. He used to draw my attention to anything natural and I'm told I was forever asking questions. I remember taking all sorts of specimens to him, plant, or animal, alive or dead, and asking him what they were. Thinking back, I remember him as knowing all the answers, but I'm sure that was not always the case! My mother was a farmer's daughter, so I guess I was destined for an outdoor life.

Apart from the biological world, we looked together at the night sky and the weather, and, on rare holidays (it was World War 2) the sea near the south Downs, where we hunted for fossils in the chalk.

I wasn't consciously connected to Nature; I just preferred to be outdoors.

Did you ever lose the connection and get out of tune with Nature?

Thankfully, I never lost the connection with Nature. I always saw Nature as it is. Nature comes naturally to me.

What effects does the connection with Nature have on your life?

The connection with Nature has always given me a great awareness and bond with the natural world. Unfortunately, this also includes sadness about the many observable adverse effects, such as the extinction of plant and animal species and extensive habitat loss, but being outdoors or observing natural phenomena, including a lot of 'green', even through a window, is still a simple pleasure.

I do not like towns and built-up places. To me the natural world is real, tangible, and unmanufactured. However, what concerns me sometimes is the fragility of Nature and the imbalance that intensive agriculture has created.

*Why do you think modern society has
lost its connection with Nature?*

When we stopped being hunter-gatherers and agriculture started, humans began to domesticate plants and animals. We made Nature work for us. Over time Nature has been used and abused for our own ends. Urbanisation also caused disconnection from Nature. And let us not forget the obsession with 'cleanliness' and 'tidiness'. Children are often not allowed to get their hands dirty or collect bugs, etc. Our lawns have to look immaculate, and grass has to be cut weekly, to maintain an unnatural coverage of land.

I still have hope though, as awareness of the importance of Nature is increasing in children. Think of the changes in the National Curriculum in the UK, for example, with lessons bringing the natural world into the classroom; then there will be the welcome introduction of a Natural History GCSE by 2025.

*In your opinion, what is the best way for
people to get in tune with Nature?*

Start young!

We raised our children with Nature in mind. Our son is a director of an outward-bound organisation and our daughter is a biologist. I sometimes think we might have overdone it a bit. We never took them to a swimming pool or a theme park, and we always went to wild places, especially the mountains for holidays. The cultural side of life was probably a bit neglected. We preferred being outdoors to visiting a museum, for instance. Although it was maybe a bit unbalanced, I have no serious regrets and am delighted that our grandchildren seem to follow in their parents' footsteps. Nature is a gift for all of us.

🌿 Meet Mel – Owner of a Zero Waste & Refill Shop and Mother of Three

Mel Hemmings is a mother of three and business owner. She runs Bare + Fair, a zero waste & refill shop in Woking, Surrey. She is passionate about helping her local community live more sustainably.

Originally, Mel studied Theatre Design at Wimbledon School of Art, and she has had various jobs including work in theatre, youth work, as a freelance artist, and working with children with special educational needs.

After a talk on climate change at the WWF Living Planet Centre in Woking, Mel got into sustainable living and although she hasn't got it nailed, she is trying to do what she can. When she came across the Zero Waste movement four years ago, she quickly realised there was need in our community for a refill shop and decided to start one herself. Mel started Bare + Fair after being at home with her small children for about 7 years, and not having had any business training or experience, it was all new to her and she has learned as she went along. When Mel is not working or busy with the family, she loves reading a good book, going for a walk or attempting to grow vegetables in her garden.

Mel is a true inspiration. She shows us that you can do anything you set your mind to. Her shop is a real paradise for Nature lovers and everyone who would like to live a sustainable lifestyle.

When did you start to connect with Nature?

As a child, my grandparents used to take me and my brothers on Nature walks, sometimes organised ones by the likes of Surrey Wildlife Trust, or sometimes just going for a walk.

My grandparents were both Nature lovers and keen gardeners, so they would often point out plants and wildlife to us. Not knowing anything else, I completely took this for granted, and it wasn't until I went to school and noticed lots of other children didn't, for example, know the names of various trees, that I had a dawning realisation of how much my grandparents had nurtured this connection with Nature in me. With my grandparents, Nature was a defining part of our relationship.

My parents also helped nurture a love of Nature in me; I have distinct memories of talking with my mum about plants while she was gardening, and my dad pointing out beautiful views on holidays. Those moments were small because of the busy family life we had, but they definitely stayed with me.

I think I also had a strong connection with Nature as a teenager. As soon as I was old enough to leave the house by myself, I would take myself off on walks in Nature on a regular basis and continued this through my teenage years; as an introvert it has always been valuable time to retreat from the chaos of life and reflect and recharge. Holidays as a teenager were often punctuated by visits to beautiful places and an appreciation of Nature in that. I took part in the Duke of Edinburgh award at school, which was a brilliant time connecting with Nature and having fun connecting with my friends. During my art studies I often came back to Nature, and I have always been inspired by it.

Did you ever lose the connection and get out of tune with Nature?

I've always felt connected to Nature, although there have certainly been times of life when I've spent less time in it or being mindful of it, because of being busy and other life priorities, like when I was a student.

The most obvious time that springs to mind was during my 20s, after leaving university, when I was very focussed on work and forging a career. There was less time in Nature and connecting with Nature during that period of my life. But it's always been a source of inspiration and even when moments of connection have been few and far between, they were nonetheless powerful.

How did you reconnect?

For me reconnecting is usually about getting back out into Nature; walking, gardening, noticing the sunset, etc. I think media sometimes has a role to play too - a good wildlife documentary never fails to remind me of the wonder of Nature, and more recently news stories about climate change and other environmental issues provide a challenging reminder of my connection to Nature and drive me to make sure it's a good connection.

What effects does the connection with Nature have on your life?

I find being connected to Nature helps me 'zoom out' mentally from the immediate demands and stresses of everyday life and is a source of peace. It inspires my outlook on life, my artistic endeavours, my work, and my spiritual life. It's something I enjoy with friends and family as well as on my own - it's an important part of my relationships. It is becoming more and more challenging though, as we are all becoming more aware of the negative effects humanity is having on Nature, and the fact that we are having to face our own responsibility in that.

I started Bare + Fair after coming across the 'Zero Waste' movement and becoming more aware of the plastic waste crisis. I was horrified by what plastics are doing to the planet and also the social justice side of the issue - that plastic waste is ruining people's homes and lives in other parts of the world. It was a paradigm shift for me, as I started thinking about some of our lifestyle and consumer choices. As we started trying to reduce our waste and plastic use at home, I found myself wishing we had a refill shop in Woking. Eventually I realised that maybe this was something I could try to do for our community, so I gave it a go and launched Bare + Fair!

Why do you think modern society has lost its connection with Nature?

I think technology and our modern lives must have a part to play in that; the rise of capitalism and consumerism is gradually separating us and distracting us from the joys and our physical connection with Nature. Our relationship with Nature is more and more becoming a source of anxiety for people, as we hear so much bad news about the state of the planet, and we must take some responsibility in our relationship with Nature. This can be hard.

In your opinion, what is the best way for people to get in tune with Nature?

I imagine it is different for everyone, but for me the introduction my grandparents gave me to Nature as a child was key, and I am in turn intentionally sharing my love of Nature with my children and others too. I think the best way for people to get in tune with Nature is through our connections with each other; whether it is experts leading guided walks, a friend sharing their love of seasonal food, a young person sharing highlights of their travels on social media, or a family going on a walk together - when you see someone else enjoying Nature, that's interesting and contagious, and not something you never grow out of. I recently met a bee farmer whose enthusiasm and knowledge about honeybees was infectious - we can always be reconnecting with Nature.

I think as a human race we tend to think of ourselves as separate from Nature, but what issues like the climate crisis and the global waste crisis are bringing into focus, is just how connected to and part of Nature we are.

❧ Meet Olivier – Naturopath, Nutritional Therapist and Naturopathic Chef

Olivier Sanchez is a registered Naturopath, Nutritional Therapist, and Iridologist. He is a published author and appears regularly on national radio shows and conferences. He specialises in stress, sleep disorders and other stress-related conditions, including gut-related inflammatory and autoimmune diseases.

Olivier is also a Michelin-trained chef with over 30 years of experience in restaurants and private employment for the rich, the famous and royalty worldwide. His vast understanding of food and his clinical experience have led him to believe that food – and stress – are the reasons behind many of the chronic diseases that are plaguing the world today.

One of the main naturopathic principles close to his heart is "Docere", which means "health practitioner as teacher." His mission is to empower people with knowledge, so they can have all the tools at their disposal to make better decisions when it comes to food and health.

When did you start to connect with Nature?

I truly connected with Nature when I was 8 years old. Aged 3, my parents decided to leave the French Riviera for the remote countryside of central France, moving from a 12-storey building to our own-built house in a rural area. We had about half an acre of land of which a third was turned into a luxurious lawn, another third was a full-sun garden, and the rest was a wild herb garden and orchard, with many established fruit trees. There was a very old pear tree that was huge and produced hundreds of pears each year. It was so high that we couldn't reach the highest branches. We had three different types of apple trees, including a surprising "Reinette Grise du Canada", which despite its name, is actually an old French cultivar of domesticated apple. We also had a hazelnut tree.

My dad took gardening very seriously. On average, we collected about

50 kg of fine green beans and peas each year. The harvest was a reason to invite our entire family and have everyone leave with their own basket. My mum would always add a few of her amazing loaves of bread and jams, and other delicacies she was so very proud to share. We were very self-sufficient.

I was quite lonely as a child. Because we came from Nice, I had a very strong accent, so when we moved to rural France, I was bullied at school. I had no friends and spent a lot of my time in the forest, climbing up trees and looking at the world from there. For me it was my world.

When I was 8 years old, I asked my dad to give me a small piece of land, right under an apple tree. To my surprise, he said yes. We didn't have a very good relationship so I guess he must have thought that it would keep me busy and quiet. I walked to nearby farms and asked for any seeds they had spare, and I started growing just about everything. Corn, wheat, courgettes, sunflowers, and anything else an excited 8-year-old boy would want to grow.

It was chaotic at times, but it was then that I started to understand the ways of Nature. If I cared for the land, then it would give back. Without realising it, gardening became a way to reach a state of stillness that I am still achieving today. Gardening is my "me-time", a type of daily 'medicine', about half an hour a day. Vegetables or berries, herbs, or plants, I am checking them daily. It is a form of meditation, a way to dissipate the constant noise of our modern lives.

I believe that when I'm connected to something, then that connection is physical. But it's also emotional, because I give my vibration to Nature and Nature gives me vibration back. For example, if I am in a bad mood, I promise you, my plants will not be happy.

Did you ever lose the connection and get out of tune with Nature?

I did indeed lose the connection with Nature when I moved to the Middle East in 2003.

During this time, I lived in a high-rise building, overlooking miles of sand-covered land. There was little availability of fresh produce and what there was, was expensive; a lettuce could cost anything over £3. Luckily, I could fly once a month to Thailand, without weight restriction, so I would bring back kilos of delicious sun-ripened fruits and vegetables at ridiculously cheap / reasonable prices. The problem was that I was no longer growing my own and I found this very difficult.

How did you reconnect?

When I moved back to the UK in 2007, I immediately bought a greenhouse, where I could grow my vegetables, even if the weather was not the best. I grew kale all year round, which quickly became a bush from which I picked the small leaves for salads and the older, harder leaves for stews and soups - it grew happily for over a decade. I also grew wild salad leaves and dandelions, away from the constant attacks of slugs and snails. The herb garden loved the British weather, and I collected organic rosemary and sage every year, drying most and grinding it into a powder that I used in all my cooking. Bay leaves and different thyme plants were also used to make my own blend of Herbes de Provence (which I use daily in all my cooking, just like garlic, shallots, and onions). Raspberries and blueberries also grew wild and were delicious.

To make sure I work with Nature and not against it, I top the soil every year with organic certified soil. I feed the plants with organic-certified seaweed-based fertilisers that help maintain the fungus-plant symbiosis. Nothing that could destroy the soil microbiota is used in my garden or pots.

What effects do the connection with Nature have on your life?

My mother cooked everything from scratch and was always experimenting with new dishes or new flavours, using home-grown produce. When I was four years old, I started to cook with my mum, and this gave me a love of good food, cooking and fresh produce. I think this and my small vegetable patch as a child influenced my career choice when I was older, to become a chef, and later a naturopathic chef.

I could not be myself or be happy if I wasn't part of Nature. I spend as much time as possible outdoors. I have recently moved to the outskirts of London, near the eastern natural reserve and I can walk for miles without seeing anyone. It is full of canals and streams, and a variety of animals and birds. It is so quiet and a great way to clear my mind. I just wish I could afford my own place with more land, so I could grow more and have chickens and bees, for example, so I could do my part in restoring balance by keeping some parts of the land untouched for bees to pollinate and other animals to thrive.

Why do you think modern society has lost its connection with Nature?

The problem with our modern society is that we have been conditioned to favour convenience to the detriment of Nature. Our tastebuds are overstimulated and, as a result, we tend to look down on healthy foods like greens and vegetables, which taste bland to the masses.

Nowadays, we pick food from shelves and aisles, without looking at what we are putting in our baskets. We buy trays of meat (most probably from a diseased, highly stressed animal that was kept indoors in poor sanitary conditions), wrapped in plastic, and injected with toxic gases, so it looks fresh and appetising, and we expect to pay as little as possible for it. We are literally facing walls of food that - for the most part - are grown for quantity and not for its nutritious qualities.

And we are surprised to find out that the nutrition profile of the fruits and vegetables sold in supermarkets is nothing compared to what it used to be half a century ago. Our food today is inadequately nutritious, because it is grown on overused and depleted lands and picked unripened, way before Nature, including the sun, could do its job.

Let's take strawberries for example. When was the last time you tasted sweet, amazing strawberries? And yet, you keep buying strawberries that are tasteless, from a plastic-wrapped plastic punnet, all year round.

In your opinion, what is the best way for people to get in tune with Nature?

The best way to get in tune with Nature is to grow something. You could start with growing anti-pollution plants. Even if you have little outdoor space or a windowsill, you can grow herbs and small plants all year round.

Use organic soil and terracotta pots. From this, you can start to experiment and grow just about anything. This year, I picked more than a dozen cucumbers from one single potted plant. I also picked handful after handful of sun-ripened raspberries and blackberries (the most amazing and largest ever), which are also in pots. From 3 strawberry plants, I now have more than 50! This year, I will donate a handful of plants because it is now too much for my small garden.

Being close to Nature is easier than you think. If you do not have green fingers, you can spend time outdoors. We are lucky in the UK to have parks and forests all around us. If you need an excuse to be surrounded by trees, then take long walks with your pet. Listening to the sounds of Nature is the best way to let go of the stress of the day and have some me-time. To reconnect with Nature and most importantly, yourself.

On warmer days, walk barefoot on the grass to ground yourself and let Nature pull away the negative ions (and emotions) from your body. There is nothing Nature wouldn't do for you, so give back. Eliminate plastic from your life and avoid as many toxic products as possible. Chose (real) eco-friendly cleaning products and detergents, or better yet, make your own. It is so easy. I have dedicated a platform to give my readers plenty of inspiration and my upcoming book will help you to make better choices when it comes to household products and reducing your exposure to pollutants and toxicants. By reducing your exposure, you are not just protecting yourself, but you are also doing your bit for the environment and protecting Nature. No step is too small. You just need to start somewhere.

🐾 Meet Orli – Nurse, Trauma-informed Massage Therapist, Writer, Artist, Dancer, and Mother to four free-spirited souls

Orli was brought up in an ordinary house, on an ordinary road, in an ordinary town, but her dreams were always extraordinary and full of fairy tales and magic.

After an encounter caring for a premature baby on a kibbutz in Israel, she returned to London, gave up her prestigious job working for a leading women's magazine, and trained to become a nurse. She worked on a Liver Transplant Unit at a large teaching hospital, before leaving to birth and raise her own tribe, latterly as a lone parent.

She introduced a trauma-informed massage service, as a volunteer, to an organisation supporting women and babies in the asylum system and became an ambassador for a leading domestic abuse charity. During the Covid pandemic, Orli worked as a Covid specialist nurse in the community, before inevitably contracting the virus during the first wave in May 2020. Her journey with Long Covid has been documented in Kate Garraway's moving TV programme, 'Finding Derek'.

By a series of synchronicities, Orli found her way to a little stone cottage high up in the remote mountains of Tuscany, totally immersed in Nature and surrounded by a ragtag pack of farm dogs, and wolves, who sang to her at night, and crystal-clear mountain rivers and endless pine forests, and by the light of the incredible full moons she finally began to heal.

In between gentle strolls collecting firewood with her magnificent wolf-dog Luna (it is unclear just who adopted who), Orli is writing a book about her experience of dancing with the 'Covid dragon', and a collection of Nature-inspired poetry. She creates art from foraged wood and shells and has been known to walk out into storms and blizzards, much to the consternation of her mountain neighbours.

Orli was introduced to me by a very dear friend, who recognised that she would be a wonderful addition to this book. I am forever grateful for this introduction, as I not only got to hear Orli's amazing story, but I also gained a beautiful friend.

When did you start to connect with Nature?

Looking back at my childhood, I have such fond memories of endless days spent in my garden when I was a little girl.

We lived just on the outskirts of London, at the top of a cul-de-sac and so our garden was huge, as it curved around the bend. I can remember being about seven years old and knowing that when the pearly white lilies of the valley were blooming underneath the holly bush, then in a few weeks the baby pink Japanese anemones would follow by the corner of the rockery and then the bright red poppies would bloom next to the Red Hot Poker plants next to the rose bushes. I knew the whole rhythm and timeframe of this garden, and in a way, this became my absolute salvation, being so totally immersed in Nature and the ever-changing seasons.

I loved collecting all the rose petals and making potions and watching the caterpillars in the greenhouse hatch into butterflies. I knew every bit of the garden and all its secrets where the tiny wild strawberries grew and the blackberries, and where the birds built their nests. It was absolutely my safe space. Just me and the secret world in the garden. I'm not sure my mother ever truly 'got it' – she used to call me 'Dolly Daydream'!

Did you ever lose the connection and get out of tune with Nature?

I think I lost the connection with Nature when I was a teenager, it just wasn't relevant to me anymore. Life was more about boys and parties and exams. And then it didn't really come back to me until more recently. Having said that, in retrospect, I guess that deep knowing was always still there, even if I wasn't consciously aware of it.

For example, when I would collect my children from school in the afternoon, instead of taking them straight home to do homework, I would drive them to a little farm, take a picnic and watch them running in

Nature. Now I can see what that was all about. But at the time it was not quite so obvious, it was more just this sort of unspoken connection.

I could see the goodness it brought them, I could see how different they were, running barefoot in the grass, as opposed to being sat in front of a TV. I had this sense of wanting them to be outside. Just seeing them coming alive and being free. Not hemmed in or cooped up in a house. I'm not sure I believe in the school system; I was always at odds with it. It was something like a necessary evil, but now there are Forest Schools and I do think, if my children had been born later, I would probably have sent them to a Forest School so they would have grown with a sense of where they belong in the world rather than in a system.

What caused this disconnection?

I think we go through phases. I left school, became a secretary, because I didn't know what I wanted to do. And then I worked in media. There was no Nature: I lived in a house, went on the train, went to this multistorey office building in central London, went home again and that was it. I don't think I saw green for years. And then, suddenly, I left and went to live in Israel on a kibbutz.

I still don't know how that even happened. I just remember going out with a friend and there was another friend there, who said she was going to this kibbutz. And I thought, I am going to do that too. My life has been a lot like that – synchronicities, leaps of faith, complete about-turns. And so, a month later, I was living in Israel, barefoot, on the most beautiful kibbutz, right on the Mediterranean. And just living this beautiful existence in Nature, in this paradise. I never wore shoes, I used to wander around in Nature, and go down to the beach every night to watch the sunset.

I lived like that for just a year because I had to come back for my mum who had suddenly fallen ill.

I came back to northwest London, to the hermetically sealed living, and I decided I was going to be a nurse, just like that. I trained at the Royal Free Hospital, and I lived at the nurses' residence nearby. And again, I don't remember very much of Nature. I went from living in the kibbutz, being utterly immersed in Nature, to no Nature, it didn't feature at all.

How did you reconnect?

The reconnection happened gradually. I got married and lived in a very 'northwest London semidetached with little garden' kind of existence but our house was opposite a beautiful park. So, at last I was connected with Nature again, but in different ways. We would take the children to Norfolk for the summers and stay in a little cottage in the middle of rolling fields, close to a remote part of the coast. I think in a way I was trying to relive the 'fairytale' of Nature through and with them. And they loved it.

And this reconnection seemed to seep out into other parts of my life too. I added Reiki and Massage Therapy to my Nursing qualifications. I looked at my patients stuck in their beds on hospital wards and realised we were just containing them and filling them full of medication. We were removing patients from anything that resembled Nature, sticking them in this concrete building. We were in effect causing a total disconnect between them and 'the source' – Mother Nature. I got into the habit, if a patient was able to walk, to walk them to the window and say "Look, can you see that tree in the distance? See how it moves? It's very windy today. Look how blue the sky is, summer is on the way". Anything to bring the outside into them.

I resigned from my post as Ward Sister because it felt like I was not doing the best by my patients. I didn't believe in the medication-only side of the treatment and the lack of any holistic informed type of input. I don't blame the staff at all – NHS nurses and doctors and all the allied teams are the unsung heroes of this world! But staffing levels were desperately unsafe and crisis management was all that was left to us. It took its toll, so I left and then set up on my own as an independent community nurse, where I could practice the kind of 'head, heart and hands' nursing for which I had come into this profession.

It became my little habit to bring into the patient's house what was going on in Nature, like "feel how cold my hands are, it is really cold out, you can feel the seasons changing" or I would bring in a little flower that I picked on the way and say, "Look the daffodils are blooming, we're back in spring again".

One of my sickest patients was in bed for a long, long time and the day that she finally managed to get out of bed, near the window, I said,

"Look outside, can you see the blossom on that tree? Can you see this? Can you see that? Look at this tree, open the window a little bit". It felt so important to her healing. it was like she had come back to life. This was the turning point. I still get very emotional thinking about that moment. All my patients survived Covid against the odds. I had oxygen set up at home for them and intravenous infusions hanging from wardrobe doors. The hospitals were overflowing, and many of my patients were elderly; this was the only hope they had. But within all the mayhem and fear, there was still time to help them remember the world outside of their beds and beyond their suffering. A world of Nature and changing seasons. The lesson is that nothing ever stays the same, not good not bad.

What effects does the connection with Nature have on your life?

I went from being this nurse that had this sense of how important Nature was for my patients, to then becoming a patient myself. In May 2020, I contracted Covid, and I went down with it heavily, as a lot of healthcare workers did, having been exposed to a very high viral load. I lost a lot of colleagues to Covid, so I know only too well how lucky I was to survive.

I spent a year in my bedroom, not being able to go out. It was just me in my bed, and my big window, looking out over the treetops. And that became my lifeline. Looking at the trees, looking at the clouds, the sunsets, the moon. During storms I used to open the windows wide, just to feel that energy. I think that was my reconnecting with Nature, including the moon cycles.

I think because every other part of my life had been stripped away, I was able to connect more deeply. And I think that when one comes face to face with one's own mortality and is allowed back again, the experience brings with it a heightened sense of wonderment and joy at the simple things in life – like the sunlight pouring in through a window or the fresh smell of the garden after a storm.

Covid nearly killed me, I couldn't even walk to the bathroom, it absolutely destroyed me. I was on home oxygen and out of my mind with pain and fear.

The first time I could physically get down the stairs, I just needed to get outside, barefoot. I put my feet in the long grass and just stood there. I do not have any words to describe that moment. I had envisioned it for so long – to be able to stand there with my feet firmly planted in the soft grass, affirming the fact that I had survived and was still very much here and alive. I actually took a picture of my feet in the grass and even now, looking at it makes me cry, because I just remember that moment in time so well.

It became my thing, whenever I could, I would just go out in the garden, if I could get down the stairs. It was a big part of my healing. There is very little else with Long Covid that heals you, other than time and grace. Sadly, there is no magic pill and very little understanding of the condition.

Almost to the day of the first anniversary of contracting Covid, I ended up on a mountain in Tuscany, in a tiny cottage in the back end of nowhere, steeped in Nature, where you hear every creak, every leaf that drops, every plant that grows. Here they celebrate Nature. They have a chestnut festival, then they have a festival for the mushrooms, and it's a beautiful thing to be somewhere where people do not only notice Nature but celebrate it and live with it in such beautiful harmony.

I had not lived like this before. When you live in London, you go to the supermarket and you can get raspberries on Christmas Day, there are no seasons. Here they taught me how to make the most of the seasons. Like at the end of summer, you pick all the basil, blend it with oil and put it in the freezer. In winter you pop a basil ice cube in your cooking, and you taste summer again.

Everything is in balance. You prepare vegetables and you use the peelings as fertilizer for the trees, nothing gets wasted.

The first cottage I lived in backed onto a tiny little smallholding, where they kept cows and pigs. I am a strict vegan, but somehow, the fact that the pigs were raised to be slaughtered before winter, didn't distress me. It didn't disturb me because everything exists here in a timeless and gentle balance. Like now, it is the wild boar hunting season, but if they did not hunt them, these boars would destroy the land and die out from disease or starvation. I'm living within an equilibrium that is so finely balanced and there is such a respect for it from the people that I'm surrounded by, they understand Nature. And this knowledge has been passed down from generation-to-generation, way back through the centuries.

Now is the time we're going to take the last of the plums from the trees and make jam for winter and collect the remaining tomatoes for bottling and pick the wild herbs from the meadows before the frosts get to them. There is a real sense of gathering in and preparing for the lack that the winter months bring.

Every time I go for a walk now, I'm bringing back firewood, because I'm aware that in a few weeks I might not be able to, as it might be raining or too cold. It is about survival, and this is new to me. But it has been my rebirth, my rewilding. Of course, there are some days that have been miserable when it has been terribly cold and like seven degrees in the house. And unless I would get out of bed and get that fire going, that's what it's going to be like all day. You get out of bed shivering, and you think, "What am I even doing here?" But then the fire gets going and you think, it is so incredibly beautiful; how lucky am I? You adapt, and you're meant to feel the seasons and live by their rules. You're meant to sleep more in the winter. It's meant to be dark, and you're meant to eat more and gain weight, and in the summer, you're meant to lose weight and feel lighter and freer. You are meant to shrink and grow with the seasons.

I don't think I can ever go back to the life I came from. I think I've tasted something that's very feral and wise and wild; and very primal. And I don't think I can ever let go of that now.

Why do you think modern society has lost its connection with Nature?

I think modern society has lost its connection with Nature because it is all about productivity. It's all about you go to school, you learn a skill to get a job, to be part of the work force, to pay for a house that you're rarely in because you're too busy working, to be able to afford it and to pay for the many unnecessary consumer-led purchases that you don't really need, but you have been led to believe you should have and somehow you get caught up in this continuum of the rat race. You go on these steel tubes underground, to get deposited off, like little worker ants and then you go out in the dark in the morning, and you come back in the dark in the evening.

And that's what it is, we must be productive. But once you break free of that, you just see what an absolute sham it all is. All that's important is that I have got enough firewood and I've I got some food in the freezer for when I run out of fresh food, and that's all that really matters. It is a million miles from consumerism. In my view, the rest of it is nonsense that we've all been fed. We have lost our way and lost sight of what's important in life. We have made it all so complicated and lost our sense of awe and simplicity and magic. And maybe nearly losing my life has made me reassess what is important and what is nonsense.

In your opinion, what is the best way for people to get in tune with Nature?

The best way for people to get in tune with Nature is to have an awareness of it.

You are never very far from Nature, even if you live in the centre of London. There's always something. Feel the grass beneath your bare feet and then you'll know your truth. That's where you literally need to start from, from grassroots. Just feel it and become more aware of what's around you. Look at the colour of the leaves, look at the moon and the stars, and once you start seeing, you will not be able to unsee it.

Your eyes have just become closed to it. We need to become children again and delight in the simple.

Start with the basics. Get a pot plant and look after it, and bring some Nature in. Keep your eyes open and start having an awareness, a gentle awareness of the world that you live in. And then it will draw you back in again to that childlike wonder you once had when you let a ladybird run over your hands and felt its tickle on your skin or blew the seeds from a dandelion clock and made a wish.

Give it a go – I promise you the magic is still there just waiting for you.

🌿 Meet Phoebe – Nutritional Therapist, Clinical Director, Product & Recipe Developer

Phoebe Liebling is a Central London-based Nutritional Therapist known for her unique approach to complex, chronic health conditions. Key to this is a focus on education and empowerment, as everyone deserves the right to understand how the choices they make will impact their health and wellbeing. In addition to her nutrition training Phoebe is also an accredited Environmental Geologist and she utilises an in-depth knowledge of the bidirectional relationship we as humans have with our natural world within everything she does. A passionate foodie, with a dedication to sustainability, organic and regenerative farming, plus a Duracell-bunny-like tendency when it comes to outdoor activity, Phoebe is very much someone who believes we exist in collaboration with our natural world, and that a detachment from this will limit our ability to be wholly well.

Phoebe and I studied Nutrition together, became great friends and whenever time allows it, we have wonderful, lively conversations. Her enthusiasm for all things related to nutrition and Nature is infectious, her knowledge is vast, and she has an amazing ability to simplify complicated processes, for all to comprehend. This book would not be complete without her.

When did you start to connect with Nature?

Looking back now, I think that I was connected with Nature from the get-go, because my mother wanted us to be outside all the time. We were only allowed to watch TV on a Saturday morning, when Mum and Dad were still in bed. They would leave a glass of milk and a biscuit in the living room, as a snack, until they would get up a bit later. But the rest of the time we were out in the garden, or on Hampstead Heath. We also walked everywhere, and we thought kids being picked up from primary school by car was the coolest thing ever. We always walked home, and we used to spend a lot of our time outdoors.

We also spent a lot of time in my grandparents' garden, picking blackberries or just mucking about.

I think that when I was little, I didn't quite realise how connected I was to Nature. We were very lucky. I still remember going to the seaside as a child, I must have been about ten years old. It was between Christmas and New Year, and my sister and I got into the sea fully clothed and just played in the sea until we were completely numb. My parents had to bring us back in the car and put us into the bath to thaw us out. We used to love doing things like that.

I think my relationship with Nature was both functional and emotional. It encouraged my sister and I to be very observant and aware of our surroundings. It also encouraged us to learn things like dexterity, when you are scrambling over rocks for instance, and how to work as a team. We were always discovering things, like picking up a crab and then finding out it was a hermit crab to be precise. We were learning to be creative and imaginative.

I grew up in Central London and we lived literally three minutes from Hampstead Heath, which is probably one of the most unadulterated park spaces that you can find.

We took the interaction with green space for granted because it was what we knew and what we did.

Did you ever lose the connection and get out of tune with Nature?

I did not really lose the connection with Nature when I got older, but there were times when I was less enthusiastic.

When it was pouring with rain, we didn't really want to go out, but my mother was still very much about taking us for a walk. There were periods of time, especially when I got older when I was not interested. For instance, when I was about fourteen years old, we were taken on a bat walk on Hampstead Heath; I was not impressed...

I think I was quite lucky because we always had dogs. When I was a teenager, my friends and I would go out dog walking. So, we had a reason to be outdoors. I think I was still connected, but I didn't realise that at the time.

My friend and I would go out for hours at the weekend, hiking around Hampstead Heath. But then there were times when the idea of having to walk somewhere for 20 minutes would seem totally unreasonable and we would semi-demand to be driven there. It was a normal teenage rebellion.

In my later teens, because I always did geography and then I went on to do geology, I spent a lot of time outside. I didn't always look forward to it, but always enjoyed it once I was outdoors.

I guess compared to the average teenagers and people in their early 20s, I spent more time outside than one naturally would do. Consequently, my proportional distaste for it was probably outweighed by the fact that I was in Nature for so long.

How did you reconnect?

When I got a bit older, I studied Environmental Geology at Leeds University and the connection with Nature became more of an academic relationship as I was outdoors for field trips. It was more of a functional interaction with Nature, less free.

It wasn't until I started travelling that I started to reconnect again.

My family has always spent a lot of time in Spain and the moment I would get off the plane and smell the air I would get this feeling of internal calm, knowing that I was going to be by the sea. Anything to do with water is just immediately calming for me, whether I'm in it, whether I'm on it, whether I'm standing next to it.

The real reconnection with Nature started again in my mid-twenties. I had become very agoraphobic because I had various digestive issues, was incredibly anxious and I just wasn't sleeping. After university I went back to live with my parents, and I used to go out for walks on my own, on Hampstead Heath. It was a solace. Just being outside in the calm, in the quiet.

I hated being around people at that point in time, I found it really difficult. Everything was over-stimulatory, like all my senses were on high alert. I found it difficult to understand what my place was, and I hated taking up space in a room. And if people were talking, even if they were talking quietly, it would sound like they were shouting. I found it all unbearable.

Going out and just hearing the calming sound of the wind in the leaves or the sound of my feet walking on crunchy bits of bark, was very soothing.

I think this was a turning point in my relationship with Nature, as a few years prior I had spent a lot of time quite intensely exercising outside, probably over-exercising due to a sense of being disconnected with myself and feeling slightly disjointed. As my digestive issues intensified, I became unable to keep this up and that frustration was definitely mirrored in a disconnect with the outdoors. Coming full circle and finding it once again as a supportive and nourishing place was incredibly important.

What effects does the connection with Nature have on your life?

The connection with Nature is integral to me, like it is a functional part of my being. When I don't have it, I don't feel well. I will get out every single morning, unless I'm exhausted and I know that I can hang out for a little bit and then go out later. I just go outside straightaway. Even when it is pouring with rain and the dog doesn't want to go outside, I'll go and stand out on the front doorstep. I just have to have that moment of pure, fresh, air.

I feel totally detached from some part of my being, if I haven't had time outside. Outdoor time can even be walking down the street to go to the tube station. It is not ideal, but it is outdoors.

In summer I will walk the dog for at least three hours a day in two blocks. Once I have done what I need to do for work, I need time to recharge, and I think that is what Nature does. For me, it gives me inner fuel, not in the sense of food but it's just like an exchange, like reoxygenation or something. It makes you feel whole again.

Sometimes when I've got something on my mind, and I'm quite stressed, I almost have a combative relationship with Nature. Because I'll try and override whatever it is that's stressing me out, by going outside, and when it doesn't make me feel better, I will then blame Nature.

It is my long-term dream to live somewhere where I could grow all of my own food.

Because there is something organic about putting your hands in the soil and watching something grow, and then being able to eat it. The full lifecycle.

I do have a tiny garden at my flat. It's a front garden. It's nothing special. I wanted a space where I could be outside as much as possible. There was something life affirming about creating something. And it gave me a level of joy that I hadn't really had in any other way.

I felt slightly addicted to it and I would be sitting on the sofa, really exhausted, thinking I could put the TV on or go outside. And I would go out in my pyjamas and wellies, until it got dark, just mucking around. I don't even know what I was doing. But I was just having a great time.

Why do you think modern society has lost its connection with Nature?

I think modern society has lost its connection with Nature, because we are no longer able to understand one stimulus at a time, we're addicted to being hyper stimulated. If you go into Nature, used to the noise, like constant music, plus being on your phone, plus having the TV on, plus doing whatever else you're doing, you can't simplify down to the organic interaction that you'd have with the natural world.

It is like giving the best raspberry in the entire world to people who have eaten loads of artificial sweeteners, they taste nothing. If you're outside, listening to birdsong or walking on fresh grass with bare feet, this will feel dull if you are used to watching David Attenborough on your Ultra HD TV whilst playing on your phone. You connect but you won't feel it.

Also, people don't give themselves time to go outside and do things. They think they're constantly busy. And they almost take it for granted if they are somewhere where there is a green space close by.

In your opinion, what is the best way for people to get in tune with Nature?

The best way to get in tune with Nature is to build a habit. You have to use active effort to start off with something, almost like a therapeutic dose of being quiet outside every single day, whether that's literally standing on your doorstep with a cup of tea and no other stimulus whatsoever, or the same in the garden or getting involved in a community project.

I think it must be something that you schedule, if it is not something you already do.

You schedule it in and be aware of not doing too many other things whilst you're outdoors.

I think you have to choose actively to do it if it is not something that you would naturally do. You wouldn't immediately go and stand outside if it is a pouring rainy day, and it's cold. But you will do it when you know how great it makes you feel.

You would have to do it for a while, starting with 10 minutes a day and making that a manageable thing. And then aim to find fun things to do in Nature, whether it's walking to a park and getting a nice coffee or finding somebody who you like to chat to and calling them on the phone while you are walking in a park instead of sitting indoors.

We know that people who spend more time in an outdoor environment have better vagal tone which makes their nervous system much more relaxed, and they're not going to be going into fight or flight nearly as much. If you're moving and walking, then you're going to be getting your lymphatic system going, so you're going to feel more energetic or have better motivation to do stuff. You're going to have less toxic burden on your body, especially if you end up breaking into a sweat. Obviously gentle movement or endurance movement, whatever you're doing, is great for cardiovascular health. I think the main thing is stress management and energy balance, blood sugar regulation from movement, but then also the exposure to natural light, which, again, is probably one of the downsides of modern living. We don't honour our circadian rhythm because we can override it with electric light whenever we want to.

And lastly, understanding seasonal eating is hugely important to connect with Nature.

The best thing that you can do is eat food that's in season. You'll get variance over the course of the year, and you'll start to understand what is good for you at different times of year. And you'll also know what we're growing right now, because otherwise there's a full disconnect.

❧ Meet Sophie – Marketeer turned Horticulturist and Mother-to-be*

Sophie Robertson is based in the East Sussex town of Lewes. She changed career from marketeer to budding horticulturist in 2019. After spending years working in an office environment, Sophie decided to make the scary, but exciting, decision to retrain. Leaving the computer screen behind, she studied at Plumpton College, which is renowned for its courses in land and environment education and is a leader for these topics in the Southeast. Achieving a distinction and the academic excellence award, Sophie became a senior gardener for a private gardening company in Brighton, followed by becoming Head Gardener for a retirement village in East Sussex, where she has overall responsibility for the gardens and grounds strategy and implementation over a 4-acre site.

I am very grateful for Sophie's contribution, as she was heavily pregnant at the time of our conversation and had only just started her maternity leave. Sophie is one of those people for whom a career change, and especially one that is close to the heart, has made a big impact on her happiness and wellbeing.

When did you start to connect with Nature?

I think I have always had a connection with Nature. I have so many memories of playing in the garden, exploring the local woods, and endless hours on the beach, when I was a child. I've also always appreciated being outdoors and how that makes you feel.

We were certainly encouraged to play outside, and we were often taken out to explore. Both my parents were busy working, so time spent together outdoors was always special, and a great way for us all to be together. I have wonderful memories of being on holiday and day trips to national parks or beautiful beaches. I think it was important for my parents to take us to places like this, to see the beauty of the world and feed our imagination!

However, I think I really began to appreciate Nature, being outdoors, growing flowers and food in 2018, when I moved into my house, which came with a beautiful garden.

A few trips to the garden centre and I was hooked! Growing what I could from seed, experimenting, seeing what vegetables I could grow, and creating a space that I loved to be in.

Did you ever lose the connection and get out of tune with Nature?

When I was a teenager, I was lucky enough to grow up in a place with woodlands close by, plenty of green spaces, and not too far from the beach, so the connection was never truly lost. My friends and I would take day trips to the sea or go for walks on the Common. However, I don't think I often stopped to take it in properly or appreciate how being in Nature made me feel. Looking back though, I am happy that my memories still have Nature in the background - it's never gone away, and I think that's a very valuable thing to have.

It wasn't until I was working in an office in the city of Brighton for a few years that I absolutely disconnected from Nature for a while. Although the beach and the downs were so close, I didn't take advantage of them being there, and life was all about going into work to be at the computer, going out to bars or for dinner and then home, most likely in front of a screen again. I can look back on that period now and say with confidence that I definitely wasn't getting any soil under my nails or going out to enjoy the great outdoors, which is a real shame, because it probably would have been just the tonic to deal with the stresses from my office job!

What caused this disconnection?

Getting stuck on that conveyor belt of working Monday to Friday, and not carving out enough time for myself. I think it's easy to get caught up in being so busy that you don't stop and think, "What's going to make me really happy right now!?". Although I was generally reasonably happy,

I don't think I really took a moment to stop and see if I had a true passion for anything.

How did you reconnect?

After falling in love with my garden, I decided to finish my job in marketing and train in horticulture. I wanted a broad view on the subject that I had fallen in love with, so I could understand it better and try to find something out there, that I could do that would make me truly happy. Being outdoors and working with plants makes me feel fulfilled and I've got a whole new perspective on Nature and what I think is important in this world.

What effects do the connection with Nature have on your life?

Whether it's eating something I've grown or being able to sit in my living room surrounded by houseplants, being connected with Nature makes me feel truly happy. If I've been outdoors for part of the day, I feel like my mood has been lifted so much more than if I would have been stuck indoors. It's such a boost for my mental health, and I also feel being around Nature helps me to feel grounded. Nothing helps you put things into perspective quite like standing by the vast ocean or surrounded by tall trees.

Why do you think modern society has lost its connection with Nature?

I think technology has a lot to do with losing the connection with Nature.

 We can use technology in harmony with Nature and it's not all bad, but I do think that modern society spends so much time living life through a screen that they forget to actually look up and take in the moment. People are also very busy all the time. Everything feels very go-go-go, and I think we need to be encouraged to stop every now and again and ground ourselves with Nature and breathe in the beauty of it all.

In your opinion, what is the best way for people to get in tune with Nature?

Just get out there! I don't think there is anything complicated people will need to do. Stop, put down the phone, put on your boots and step outside. Whether you live in the city or the countryside, there is Nature out there to explore.

I love that people are finding a passion for houseplants too. Just one little plant in your bedroom can make the world of difference. We share our home with over 100 houseplants, so I'm a big advocate for bringing the outdoors inside. It's especially comforting when the weather is miserable, and you can't go outdoors. People can also try growing something. You don't need a garden; you can grow basil on a windowsill. It's so rewarding sowing a seed and watching it transform. I believe that gives you a whole new appreciation for plants.

*Since I spoke to Sophie, she and her husband have welcomed a beautiful baby girl, named after a flower.

🌱 Meet Susan – Acupuncturist, Chinese Herbalist & keen ice-skater

Susan Adams grew up in the predominantly Scandinavian state of Minnesota, USA, but during her childhood and teenage years she was surrounded by East Asian friends, and this is when her interest in those cultures began.

After graduating with a BA in Religious Studies, and in Middle Eastern Area Studies from the University of Minnesota, she worked in organic food cooperatives and developed a passion for whole foods. After years of living in Europe and travelling through Israel, India, and China, she ended up in Japan, where she met her British husband and moved to the UK in 2003. Susan has a thriving Chinese Medicine practice in Woking, UK.

I first met Susan many years ago, when she was working in a holistic clinic in Woking.

We became friends and have been working together since I started my own nutritional therapy practice. She is a very knowledgeable, interesting, and warm human being, and a wonderful acupuncturist with a great deal of interest in the natural world.

When did you start to connect with Nature?

To me, Nature means being outside and feeling the seasons, experiencing the air, land, water, and looking at the sky. How I adapt to my surroundings emotionally and physically is my internal connection to Nature. When I go outside, I try to erase my judgements about the weather. I love a memory of being in university when it was -20°C. I used to take off my shoes, put on very thick woollen socks, and walk on the icy snow. I would hear and feel crunching under my feet, and a crisp bite of the frozen air on my face. No one was ever outside, so the silence was thick in the frigid air, making the cracking underfoot really loud.

Even though I never lived in the countryside, as a child I immersed myself in Nature. I played in the deep snow, swam in pools during the scorching summers and slid down grassy hills during pounding thunderstorms. I spent hours sifting through rocks lining the car park at the playground to find special ones, collected tadpoles in the stream behind the playground, and built extensive tunnels, ramps, and sculptures from the sticky snow. When the temperatures dropped, the glide of the sled whirred on the crystalised snow texture. The seasons were also marked by a few harvests; in the summer my grandma would send us a crate of peaches, which I would gorge on, and in the autumn, I ate sweetcorn until I felt sick. It was almost like I knew the time was limited to eat those things.

Later, as a young adult, I craved being in urban environments, where I could walk around and look at people. I felt a connection with the Nature of the people I saw and met.

Did you ever lose the connection and get out of tune with Nature?

I think I had a break with Nature when my parents had relationship issues when I was around 4-5 years old. My mother had mental health problems and it seemed like a sort of internal natural disaster was happening in my life. I think Mom had postnatal depression, and I would say that it broke my childhood connection with Nature and of being care-free. I had been able to wake up and go outside with my four siblings with a purpose relating to the season, whether playing baseball or building a snow ramp. With the problems at home, I felt a need to leave the house, to be with friends, especially when I was about 11-14 years old.

A distinct disconnection happened to me at my first female "life gate", when I was about 13 or 14 years old, around the time I started to have periods and change to a very large junior school, where the children were mean. There was the confusion of being around a lot of people I didn't know or feel comfortable with, and suddenly not being a kid anymore.

Later on, in my mid-twenties while travelling around Europe, I felt disconnected too, as I was so busy being in different places, that I had no roots, like a plant that can't grow once cut. In my 4 ½ years in the concrete metropolis of Tokyo, I felt a split with Nature when taking the overflowing trains to my workplaces. Now, when I drive too much, I notice a longing for being outside, so this disconnect still happens to me.

How did you reconnect?

Around age 9 I spent a lot of time with one Vietnamese immigrant family, and it felt like I was travelling abroad when I was with them. They spoke no English at the time, but somehow, we communicated. It was a significant time when I was immersed in another culture that I had no opinions about. I smelled new aromas and ate new food, which hadn't existed in my life, and this was a part of Nature. I realised I wanted to see more of the world. Being free to move and travel became an important part of my life, not to have roots in one place was what I longed for.

My first time living away at 18, I went to the University of Minnesota, Duluth (UMD) which is a campus connected by tunnels. Escaping those tunnels into the frigid outdoors was amazing in Duluth. I was enrolled into a private school, about half a mile down the road at St Scholastica University because all Spanish classes were full at UMD. I had to walk there, and it ended up being the best thing for me because the buildings at St Scholastica looked European and it felt like I was travelling, going down the road in the freezing air with walls of snow drifts.

Duluth is on Lake Superior which is the biggest freshwater lake in the world. It has waves, and even tides, and is smack in the middle of the US, yet reaches the Atlantic Ocean. I used to walk down to the port to get away. I loved walking there, sitting on the rocks and looking at the ships that had just come from far away countries.

I transferred to the Minneapolis campus of the university. It's an expansive place and I had to walk across the Mississippi River to get to some classes. That river has an immense power, and I never lost my respect for its depth and size. Around that time, in my 3rd year at University in Minneapolis, I bought a mountain bike and decided I wouldn't use any public transportation until I paid off my new bike in the distance I rode. That was fantastic because I rode it in the summer, in deep snow, on ice, and in the rain. I got back that deep connection with my environment from when I was young.

After graduating, I was an au pair in Mallorca and a nanny in Paris, then travelled to European capitals, India, and China spending hours every day wandering the streets on my own, no matter the weather. I didn't see Nature so much or connect with people, but I just explored. I was on a kibbutz in Israel for 3 months and spent a lot of time outside on the mountain-based commune which overlooked Lebanon and an Israeli town below. I took a real interest in the history and the peoples' stories, which helped me connect to the area.

In Tokyo I bought a scooter and shipped my mountain bike there from the US and connected with my environment really well by being outside in any weather and enjoying exploring and feeling the fresh air every day. I lived in Hiroshima for 6 months and will never forget the spectacular shift from concrete to mountains, trees, and beautiful architecture. I would hop on my little scooter and chug up to the top of a pine covered mountain to get to a Shinto shrine and just relax, looking at the gardens on my own.

Around 5 years ago I realised that since leaving Minnesota in 1996 I've missed very cold winters, with ice and snow. At my third "life gate", menopause, I decided it was important for me to do ice skating seriously and I joined an ice hockey team. The only problem is that it's indoors and doesn't fully connect me back to Nature.

Even now reconnecting with Nature is a work in progress. Meditation helps me a lot, particularly when I go on a Vipassana retreat. Looking at the clouds is soothing and humbling.

What effects do the connection with Nature have on your life?

I think of connecting with Nature as a solitary experience. When I look at the clouds, I feel happy and relaxed. I feel connected with the present moment. This connection helps to erase lots of clutter from my brain.

I became a vegetarian when I was 20 years old, very much in the hope of having less of an impact on animal suffering. Often when I think of the ideas of how the connection of Nature affects my life, I remember discussions about global warming and the dying out of species of animals and plants. How I can impact these things is confusing. There are so many theories about what is good for our world, from meat being bad for the environment to needing animals to nourish the soil to grow things. It's difficult to feel like I'm doing something to improve the physical environment in a significant way, but it brings me closer to Nature when I'm conscious of eating good food.

When I am connected to Nature, I have a sense of inner calm and connectedness. I get a sense of better health generally.

Why do you think modern society has lost its connection with Nature?

Modern society has lost its connection with Nature because of distractions, the very detailed and complicated processes we all have, the hectic schedules and perceived expectations from others. We just get caught up in the stream of life and don't step onto the shore to have a wider look. For me, this is mindfulness. We may be in an urban environment or in the countryside, but it's all the same planet and there is Nature everywhere, we only need to notice it.

In your opinion, what is the best way for people to get in tune with Nature?

The best way to get in tune with Nature is to stop. Take some time off, just for yourself and ask that question – regularly. I think there may be different answers for everyone.

But whatever you do, make it easy. Find a herb and chew on it. Smell a flower. Just start to find those things each day. Use all your senses. Use food because that is part of Nature. Have a nice, fresh bowl of soup: smell it, look at it, feel it, and taste it. Make it super accessible.

❧ Meet Thinley – Bhutanese Traditional Medicine Practitioner

Thinley Om is from Bhutan, the country known for the Gross National Happiness philosophy.

Thinley holds a degree (BSc) in Traditional Medicine from the Faculty of Traditional Medicine, Khesar Gyalpo University of Medical Sciences of Bhutan. She started her career as a Resident Traditional Chinese Medicine (TCM) Doctor in 2017 with the Bhutan Spirit Sanctuary, a 5-star traditional spa-inclusive resort situated in the Paro valley. She also worked as a visiting practitioner and wellness consultant at Kagi Resort in the Republic of Maldives. Thinley currently works as a wellness expert at a resort in Bali, Indonesia.

When I first met Thinley, she impressed me with her gentle manner and wealth of knowledge and when I started to get to know her more, I learned that she is a well-balanced and grounded person. We talked at length about wellness and traditional medicine, mindfulness, and nutrition, we just clicked, both of us being passionate about natural healing. Thinley also shared with me information about a research project she was doing on Forest Bathing, the simple method of being calm and quiet amongst the trees, observing Nature around you whilst breathing deeply.

When I was looking for the right person to have a conversation with on 'The Lost Connection with Nature', she immediately sprang to my mind. Here is Thinley's story.

When did you start to connect with Nature?

From my childhood, or as early as I can remember, I started to connect with Nature. I used to go into the forest with my parents to collect firewood, and dried leaves for our cattle at home. Initially, it was just a physical connection, and I cannot recall any spiritual, mental, or emotional connection; I was just helping my parents. But as I grew older, I realised the importance of the forest, since we depended heavily on it for our livelihood, and the reasons for considering the natural environment around us as so sacred: the trees, stones, streams and so on.

When I experience hardship in life, I turn to Nature for healing, help, and companionship. Similarly, if I'm bored, anxious, or upset, I remember and recall my deep connection with Nature. These experiences helped me choose a career as a 'helper', for those who seek a helping hand, or simply long to share their stories.

My bond with Nature has always been my greatest companion, and I do recommend others (if interested), to forge a relationship with Nature to help themselves, not only when suffering from overwhelming thoughts and emotions, but also when facing so many mental disorders or draining energy.

I like to get lost in Nature, smelling flowers and herbs, working with my herbal teas, and listening to the chirping sounds of birds and insects. It gives me happiness and recharges me physically, mentally, and emotionally. The more I enjoy my profession, the more I enjoy my connection with Nature. And you'll see the beauty of co-existence for yourself.

I can now understand why holy practitioners or learned teachers can stay in the mountains for years and years, deep in meditation and prayer, relying on Nature.

I would also like to mention our thoughts and emotions here. We are, after all, what we think.

We are slaves of our emotions and thoughts, and I totally agree with His Holiness the Dalai Lama on what he says about calming one's mind:

"…to have a clean body, you must have physical hygiene, and more significantly to have a clear mind; hygiene for emotions and thoughts is an important step"

"Emotional hygiene is needed to wash away the negative emotions that are clouding our mind. Nature is the best place to do that."

Choosing Nature as your true companion is the best companionship, as it is committed and trustworthy.

*What effects does the connection with
Nature have on your life?*

In a few words: self-healing, self-belief and being a better person.

Believing in myself was something that Nature instilled in me.

I am from Bhutan, a small Kingdom in the great Himalayas. I am a farmer's daughter, who has not travelled beyond Bhutan until recently, and I had to take on a lot of responsibilities at a young age.

Embarking on a journey to obtain a degree of Bachelor of Science in Traditional Medicine and joining the wellness hospitality, were challenging, but I always had my greatest friend, Nature.

I have a passion for what I do. I describe my job as being a Listener, who listens to my guests' or patients' story, being part of it and helping them with my simple yet profound healing.

Healing oneself and our personal development are also important and should be practiced, hence, the question, "Are you ready to listen and heal?" The answer is, "Yes", if you're doing both.

During my journey I have met hundreds of people from different parts of the world and now I am here in Bali, sharing my story, a decision I took back in 2016 along with my trustworthy companion, Nature.

*Why do you think modern society has
lost its connection with Nature?*

Due to changes in people's mindset and lifestyles, more and more people, in almost all parts of the world, are experiencing mental health issues from a very young age. Stress, anxiety, depression, dysfunctional relationships, etc. are being experienced by many people, not just the young ones.

Pills, supplements, herbs, talking to a therapist or psychiatrist is often not enough.

Self-reflection could be helpful, and Nature is a good place for this, without any distraction.

When my parents were young, there was less technology and more human interaction, with good conversations and time spent together. Nowadays we don't even have an idea who is living next door, and even within families the connections are not that strong anymore. We don't have time to sit together and have our meals with family, even if we are all home.

People are lost in the digital world and many conversations take place on social media channels such as Messenger, Instagram, and Facebook. Human connection and especially our connection with Nature are lost and it is high time that it bounces back for wellness.

In your opinion, what is the best way for people to get in tune with Nature?

Getting connected with Nature is simple. Start with something basic and simple. Perhaps nurturing a flower plant at home, or just planting some mint and preparing your own herbal tea. This process is simple, doable, and can definitely take you to higher levels, connecting with Nature. Your hands in the soil, nurturing and watering your plant, and sharing the positivity, will give you the best ever tea, that is between the simple mint and you.

Being mindful is also a good start, as mindfulness enhances our ability to connect with Nature. Your mind needs to be still for a moment, and everything will be possible, for we are the most fortunate living creatures on earth, as we have the potential to think logically, understand the situation, and make the right decision. Experiencing this yourself, with the right approach, will get you to another level of wellness, happiness, and harmony.

🌿 Meet Tone – Chiropractor, Founder of Luck's Yard Clinic and Co-founder of The Green Hub Project for Teens

Tone Tellefsen-Hughes was born in California, USA, of Norwegian parents. The family moved back to Scandinavia when she was four years old, and they settled north of Stockholm, in Sweden. By the age of four she spoke 3 languages. Tone is a chiropractor, who has practiced in the UK for 29 years. She runs a multi-disciplinary chiropractic clinic in Surrey and is also the Co-Chair of a community organisation called the Green Hub Project for Teens. They offer Nature-based therapy sessions for teenagers aged 13-18 in a magical secluded, walled garden behind the practice. The project started in 2021 and they have had over 35 teenagers go through a 12-week programme in the first 18 months of being open. Tone is also a workshop leader and has a passion for helping teens find their own power and inner strength. She loves being outdoors, walking in Nature and swimming in her local river.

When did you start to connect with Nature?

I started to connect with Nature as soon as I was born. My father was a scout leader until he was into his twenties, and he was very keen for us to be close to Nature too. This meant lots of walking in the woods, foraging, canoeing or just hanging out in Nature.

My father was also a physicist and a very spiritual man, he introduced me to tree-hugging.

We lived in a leafy, suburban area in Sweden, so we had plenty of Nature around us.

In Sweden, all year round you do lots of activities in Nature, such as swimming in the summer in the lakes, and skating, cross country skiing and down-hill skiing in the winter.

I was also very fortunate that my grandparents had a cabin on the south coast of Norway. It was very rustic and primitive, with no running water. We had to walk over a field to get there, and we spent every waking hour outside, running on cliffs and swimming in the sea.

Watching the storms roll in, with lightning at sea, made me very respectful of Nature.

Skiing in the mountains gave me an overwhelming feeling of how old and strong the mountains are, and how small we are in comparison.

Nature has always been incredibly important to me. My connection with Nature as a child was not just a physical experience, but thanks to my father, also an emotional and spiritual one. It was a relationship that I never lost while I was a teenager, as life continued with gardening, walking and being outdoors.

Did you ever lose the connection and get out of tune with Nature?

The only time I lost the connection with Nature was when I lived in a flat in Stockholm for two years after graduating. I hated it and I vowed never to live in a flat again if I could avoid it. We lived on the fourth floor, and I missed the lack of connection with the ground. I was literally bouncing off the walls of the flat.

When I studied chiropractic on the English South coast for four years, we lived near the sea, and I had to go down to the water several times a week just to connect to the big body of water. This meant a lot to me.

How did you reconnect?

When I moved back to the UK and to Surrey, we bought the tiniest house, but we did have a garden. I created my own vegetable patch for the first time ever and I loved it.

The house was also surrounded by trees, and there was this magical woodland across the road, which would lift my spirits immediately when I walked there. All the roads near the house were covered with a canopy of trees, like a tunnel. The way to work was literally covered in trees. It was so beautiful; I was in heaven on the way to work. When we moved to a bigger house, we only moved a few hundred yards from this area, so we still have the magical woodlands near us. I will never stop loving this area, and I will not take it for granted.

What effects do the connection with Nature have on your life?

Nature has so many effects on my life.

A few years ago, I felt strongly that there was something missing in my life and that I was longing for daily contact with Nature. I wanted to be in the woods and exercise in some way every day. We then got our Ridgeback puppy Pluto and we decided to do all our own walking with him. I am now in the woods at least twice, 5 days a week, and I would say that I walk or hike with him up to 8-10 hours a week. So, I have worked hard to realise a dream and it has really changed my life and given it a new meaning.

When I am walking in Nature, I can see and follow the changes of the seasons. When I am in my little vegetable patch, I feel stress literally running out of my body and into the ground. It helps me to be more mindful and present. I also get lots of creative ideas in Nature, which help me for my work and our charity. What I love about Nature and gardening is that it just accepts you for who you are.

Four years ago, I read the book, 'Lost connections' by Johann Hari. It follows him travelling around the world, to find out why people are depressed. In the book he is talking about a social prescription surgery in East London. They started a community garden in a forgotten patch of wasteland. The group of volunteers who go there gradually got to know and care about each other, and their depression eased. After reading this book, I had the opportunity to lease a small, walled garden behind my practice. We have since created a community organisation called The Green Hub Project for Teens that offers Nature-based therapy for teenagers who are struggling with stress, anxiety, and depression. This book literally changed my life, as I now am part of a tribe of wonderful volunteers who I am connected with and who all help young people connect with themselves in Nature.

More recently I travelled to Norway, and we crossed the Sognefjord to visit the oldest stave church. While I was standing on the deck, in the rain, looking out over the fjord, I felt a deep sense of peace, and it was very calming and grounding. These experiences have enriched my life and I am so grateful for them.

We have tried to instil the importance of Nature into our children. Every summer we spent time in Sweden, on Gräsö island in the Baltic Sea, and at home we spent time in our garden and went for walks in Nature. There is a Swedish saying that there is no such thing as bad weather or clothing, so we are out in all weathers. Our eldest daughter is a llama trekker, and she works outdoors in Nature, connecting with animals. Our other daughter is studying geography and geology, so her professional life will most likely be literally studying Nature itself.

Why do you think modern society has lost its connection with Nature?

There is a strong power that keeps people from being outdoors and in my opinion, this is the draw of the internet, smart phones, and gaming. When we were little, we didn't have these options, so we would go outside. Our parents didn't drive us everywhere and didn't fill our lives with organised activities as parents seem to be doing today. We just had to go outside and figure out what to do. We cycled everywhere. In today's society we are expected to be incredibly busy all the time and do everything fast.

However, slow-paced living is gaining momentum and there are now more people who are trying to do less and do it slower. But it is a new way we all have to find.

In your opinion, what is the best way for people to get in tune with Nature?

To get in tune with Nature, start with something achievable. It has been shown that just sitting on a bench in a park changes your mood. If you sit with someone else this effect is even more powerful.

Try to do your meetings while walking outside. Again, research has found that walking meetings create more ideas and thinking outside of the box.

In hospitals they have found that those patients who had Nature pictures on the wall, got better sooner than others. Those who had a window looking out on a park got better even faster.

Maybe try to move your desk so that you can see Nature from your window every day.

Plan Nature time in your weekly schedule. My mother, who still works in her 80s, schedules exercise in her diary first, then work. Why not do the same with Nature?

Make it a non-negotiable activity in your life. Don't ever let it slip.

Having a dog, who must be walked twice a day, makes this an easier option.

Maybe borrow a dog, just so it makes you get out. Being accountable can help make this a daily activity.

🌿 Meet Victoria – Director of Silverwoods Forest School and Mother of One

Victoria Hofgartner is the Director of Silverwoods Forest School in Surrey. She is also mother to a very happy and confident little boy.

Victoria is creative and passionate, inspiring children and adults that attend her forest school to be more in tune with Nature. She feels that everyone needs Nature and the great outdoors in their life; it feeds the soul. She is a qualified Forest School Practitioner and has several years' experience working as a nanny with children of all ages. Victoria works with various local schools and has helped in the running of forest school sessions for four Forest Schools across Surrey and London. She also has experience working with children with disabilities and special educational needs. It is her aim that children become more independent learners, whilst having a good understanding of the woodland world around them.

Victoria is very passionate about Wild Food and how we can forage sustainably in the wild.

She is currently studying, "Teach Foraging" at the Wild Harvest School.

When did you start to connect with Nature?

I started to connect with Nature from a young age. I was born in 1984 and I suppose parents back then were probably a bit more laidback with letting their children play outdoors.

I think in those days it was a bit safer than it is now. So, I was always off on my bike. I was lucky that we lived near wooded areas. We would be out, without mobile phones, riding around with all our friends and we would have to be back before dark, in time for our tea.

We have always been out in Nature as a family. That's where it all started.

When I was young, it was probably a more physical connection with Nature. Now I am more spiritually connected, as I've got older and wiser. It takes a while for your eyes to open and actually see the benefits of really looking at Nature. I'm thinking of mycelium for instance, the root-like structure from which mushrooms grow, an ecosystem, that you can even find on a tiny little patch of ground. Just sit there and look at it, it's alive. Most people walk past it, and they don't notice little things like that.

We are trying the same approach with our 5-year-old son. My husband and I are both outdoorsy people so we're always out. We don't go to soft play places or anything, as long as there is woodland nearby, we're outside and we'll go for walks. It doesn't have to cost money, Nature is free, and you should go out and utilise it.

Did you ever lose the connection and get out of tune with Nature?

During my teenage years the connection with Nature was not so strong. I guess the hormones were running wild.

How did you reconnect?

My husband was the one that pulled me back into Nature. He is much more outdoorsy than I am. He is from France, where his family run a fishery. They are living in their little bubble, with two big lakes and lots of woodland, so right in the middle of Nature.

We have been going there for a good 10 years now, to visit the family and for long holidays, being outdoors all the time. My husband taught me how to fish and taught me a lot about wildlife. That's when I started to do more research and really got into all things Nature.

I studied travel and tourism at college, but that was not my aspiration. I think I was far too young to know what I wanted to do. I didn't really know until I did my Forest School course in 2015.

I had been in childcare for some time, working as a private nanny and because I worked with children, a friend told me about forest schools. I did a bit of research and really liked what I found out. A job that takes me outdoors would fit very well with the sort of life I was hoping to be heading for. In 2015 I did the forest school practitioner level three course, and I haven't really looked back since. I am working in three primary and infant schools, as well as running my own private Silverwoods Forest School.

Forest school aims to inspire and encourage all individuals of any age, gender, and background, to enjoy the freedom to explore the natural world through positive outdoor encounters, in all seasons and weathers. It is an innovative approach, that provides opportunities to achieve and develop confidence and self-esteem through hands-on learning experiences in and around a woodland or natural environment.

What effects does the connection with Nature have on your life?

Other than being able to be outdoors because of work, the connection with Nature is also great for my mind. Whenever I am feeling stressed, I just want to get into the woods, and I feel the stress melting away very quickly. I personally think it is because of all the colours, especially the green. It is hard to put into words. Nature is about touch and smell, it is sensual. I am a quite tactile person, and I always get soil under my nails, etc.

Being out in the calm, listening to the birds and the wind in the trees, even if it's raining or freezing cold, it all has its own beauty.

I feel like I'm more in tune and connected with the seasons as well, because I'm outdoors all the time. And it has an effect on my physical health too. Touch wood, I haven't been ill for ages. Not even a cold. I think it undeniably boosts your immune system.

The trees release phytoncides, which increase the numbers of natural killer cells in the body, improving the immune response. They also have an anti-inflammatory effect.

There is a great saying by Edward Abbey, "Wilderness is not a luxury but a necessity of the human spirit".

Why do you think modern society has lost its connection with Nature?

Why has modern society lost its connection with Nature? Where do we start?

I think we live in such a materialistic world. It's all about fast fashion or the latest gadget or gizmo. Everyone is quite engrossed in their phones. A lot of people are constantly looking down and not really looking, like the people who walk into a lamppost, like zombies, while on their phones. I think technology has a big part to play in our loss of connection with Nature. But I'm not going to slate technology too much, because obviously it also has its bonuses. Where would we be without it?

In my view greed is part of the problem too. Just watch the adverts on TV. I just think there is too much commercialism. And there is the issue of safety. Parents often think it's not safe to let their children out, so they would rather keep them indoors, in their bedroom, with their PlayStation. Luckily, I lived my childhood in a different time. Nowadays, a lot of children are gaming or on their phone. That's how they communicate.

In your opinion, what is the best way for people to get in tune with Nature?

One of the best ways to get in tune with Nature is forest bathing.

A lot of research has been done, especially in Japan. Forest bathing is basically being calm and quiet amongst the trees, observing Nature around you, while you are breathing deeply.

It can help you to de-stress and boost your health and wellbeing in a natural way, without pills.

I would say start by going outdoors. Look at the weather forecast and dress appropriately in the right clothing. And then just go for a walk, even if it is in your local park or green space.

Put away your mobile phone and start being more present and mindful about what you're doing. See how many different species of birds you can spot. Don't stress yourself out too much if you don't know what they are.

We will also need to slow down a bit more because life is hectic. It's important that we are mindful about what we are doing. It is hard if we are in the rat race, because that's the system we live in. It is hard to get out of the system completely and live off the land.

In my view, just having an understanding that you need to be outside in Nature will help, a deep understanding about the connection. It won't happen overnight, it takes a while, and you have got to embrace it and trust it. But I think when people know about the health benefits, such as getting vitamin D from sunlight even when the sun is not shining, it will happen.

And of course, it needs to be on the government's agenda to educate children on Nature's benefits when they're young.

🌿 Meet Zarah* – Trauma Survivor and Nature-lover

When Zarah (*not her real name; she would like to remain anonymous given the sensitive nature of her story) is not working, you can find her outdoors in her garden, in the woods or with her dogs, chickens and bees. Before her current job, she worked as an outdoor instructor which sparked her love for outdoor activities like climbing, diving, and caving.

Zarah is very much in tune with Nature, and has always been, even though her work sometimes disrupts her natural rhythm, but she always makes sure to get back to Nature to find balance. Her garden is her gym and her haven, and it gives her the peace and quiet she craves so much. She is a member of the Wildlife Trusts, World Wildlife Fund, National Trust, RSPB, Bumblebee Conversation Trust and various other local charities related to Nature.

Apart from the fact that I have always known Zarah to be a serious Nature lover with green fingers and a great affinity for animals, it is also her story that made me decide to ask her to participate in this book as it shows the profound healing of Nature more than anything. I am immensely grateful that she is brave enough to share her story as I know how difficult it is for her.

When did you start to connect with Nature?

My earliest memories are of being outside, in a garden, eating a tomato, and enjoying the sense of freedom. I must have been around four years old. All my memories from then are of being in awe of flowers and insects, especially ladybirds (of which there were many then).

My real connection came a little later, I must have been about 5 or 6 years old, when we moved to an isolated area in the West Country, into an old cottage. There were only 6 other houses, and nothing but fields and coastline. The houses were where the Council tended to place more problematic people. My parents, and especially my mother, were not conventional in any shape or form.

My parents divorced and I was left with my mother and stepfather. They were alcoholics and drug addicts. My childhood was full of abuse of every kind. It was a lonely existence, but the one constant was Nature. I was able to escape at times. Build dens, try to help Nature (I used to walk around looking for injured animals) walk the coastline, investigate wildlife by looking under rocks, in hedges, ponds, etc.

Did you ever lose the connection and get out of tune with Nature?

I have always felt a connection with Nature, even when I ran away to the big city, when I was 17 years old. My connection with Nature had been reinforced through the years and when I was taken into the city, I felt overwhelmed and frightened by the lack of Nature. The smell, in particular, was overpowering. I remember loving the big roundabouts, as they were one of the few places that seemed to be green. I grew up with a fear of cities, and it is something I still have today, but in a more mature way. The ever-sprawling concrete. So, to escape the city, I spent much of my time going out to Dartmoor and finding new and wild places.

I would just take myself off for a walk, getting completely lost and ending up finding all sorts of weird and wonderful places. Before I ran away to the city, I would walk for miles, but I always knew exactly where I was, and I had the place to myself. This is one of the things I'm missing now, I can't walk, get lost and not see people. I'm very selfish and still want the place to myself, being close to Nature.

Even when I'm in Central London I marvel at something trying to grow through the cracks, like a Buddleja that is constantly growing out of the sides of buildings, and that is what I did in the past too. But mostly it was taking myself off and walking the path that other people hadn't walked. It was fantastic, it really was.

I didn't know many like-minded people during that time. I like my own company, but I had also left college quite abruptly because I had a disagreement with the lecturer and the students. I didn't have much of an education because I spent much of my time looking after my half brothers and sisters. And I had some major trauma when it came to my exams as well. So, my grades weren't fantastic, and I didn't have many prospects, career advice was hopeless at the time. I ended up doing a family and community care course and on the Friday afternoons we were doing arts & crafts at the same time as a group of teenage boys with learning disabilities. My class consisted predominantly of girls, and they were continuously teasing and making fun of these boys, and I think, because I had gone through some pretty traumatic times of humiliation, etc. myself, to see these boys being humiliated was just the final straw for me.

So, I impulsively left college as I didn't want anything to do with these people. At the same time, I was volunteering, working with mentally disabled people, and I was asked to help on an outdoor activity week away. And that is when I met likeminded people, outdoor pursuits people that were into climbing, caving and being in touch with Nature in that way.

This experience made me decide to become an outdoor instructor, for which I trained when I was about 20 years old. I also trained as a diver medic technician which involves administering medical aid and life support skills and taking people into hyperbaric chambers for oxygen therapy. Not just divers who were sick, but also cancer patients and people suffering from gangrene.

After all that I worked for a few years as a residential therapist at a private boarding school for boys with behaviour problems, taking them outdoors for physical activities such as hiking, climbing, caving, but also taking them to theme parks, farms, etc. The boys showed excellent behaviour and it was very rewarding; it clearly showed that taking them outdoors changed their behaviour and gave them freedom. I eventually left when the management changed, and the boys weren't getting enough of the educational therapy they needed so badly.

Life changed a lot when I met my husband and I realised that after all those years of working with people I had had enough and wanted to get away from people, be more creative. So, I retrained which at the time seemed like a good idea. I don't know why, but I do have a bit of regret that I somehow didn't end up in horticulture or something like that. It is a pity that at school botany was not a subject, so young people would be more likely to choose a career in horticulture. I did Rural Science at school and that was my favourite subject. Nowadays GCSE Agriculture and Land Use is offered as a subject, which is important as we need more farmers. I'm thinking, once I retire, to retrain in horticulture through a non-age-restricted apprenticeship.

Although I like my current job, especially the creativity, there are aspects that I find quite hard, like sitting in a car and spending hours driving in Central London.

The job is also incredibly humbling, seeing the terrible conditions some people live in and the homelessness, especially in London. It is very worrying, also because you can't expect people living in those sorts of conditions to think about climate change or think about protecting Nature, when it is not around them and survival or self-preservation are the only things that are on their mind. It really humbles me and makes me appreciate what we have.

The fact that my job involves working irregular hours - it is almost like shift work - is not always easy for me as it disrupts my body clock. I'm very much an early bird, I'm awake naturally, between 5 and 6am, every morning, so I do struggle with late shifts.

I have to balance it all with Nature at home. I have got plants everywhere in the house, I try to take the dogs out and do something in the garden every day.

What effects does the connection with Nature have on your life?

My connection with Nature has been my therapy, my escapism. I truly believe that it saved me, as I tried to take my own life when I was 10 years old, and would probably have tried again, had I not had the wildness to escape to.

I find it difficult today to find that wildness. I found it particularly difficult during Covid, when the world decided to get a dog and walk in protected areas, letting their dogs foul, rampage through nesting areas, and leave litter (coffee cups and masks). I found it very hard to witness and ended up spending most of my time in my garden, which I am very fortunate to have, in order to avoid seeing the destruction.

Nature is also my gym. Apart from hiking, caving, etc., I do a lot of things manually when I am working in my garden. We do own a lawn mower and use it sometimes, but for my wildflower patches I use a scythe and for the hedges I often use shears instead of a hedge trimmer. Instead of going to the gym and paying to use my muscles, I use my muscles in the garden. It is more environmentally friendly, and less noisy! There are so many people that will get electrical, or petrol driven tools that do jobs for them.

Why do you think modern society has lost its connection with Nature?

I think there are many reasons for this.

Society has always been influenced by image, but with social media even more. People are often more concerned with the aesthetics of their gardens, than the benefits that their gardens could give to wildlife. They want the manicured lawns. The 6-foot fence to seal themselves in. The weeded, bare soil shrubbery. What is bizarre is that people create gardens like this, then go for walks and post pictures of how wonderful some wild area is, not realising that their garden could be a wild area. This Victorian style of gardening is taking its toll on wildlife. I hear my neighbour's leaf blower all the time, he has a constant battle with the many leaves that flood his garden, he used to burn them, but he has now been convinced to leave them in his woods, and I will even take some from him for composting or layering the beds. He is constantly carving his own trees with a chain saw and wants to chop branches from my tree which is full of ivy and nesting areas because his 'grass isn't growing in that corner', he puts poison down for the mice. The soil around his plants is bare and lifeless.

I also think it is about education and this is where social media is slowly starting to help. Many children have grown up or are growing up without any contact or education on Nature, conservation, and environment. If we don't have green spaces, how can people appreciate them? Sure, we have parks, etc., but they are mostly devoid of Nature due to their size, and they lack wildlife pathways to other green spaces. Many children are growing up without a sense of wonder and awe about Nature and rely on media to fill the void. They may watch a David Attenborough Nature documentary or other wildlife programs, but without getting out there and experiencing it, they are desensitised to it.

Education, gardening programmes and groups have been really slow to advocate for wildlife/Nature. Many people really do not understand the benefits of planting native plants and trees and creating or protecting Nature. I still see gardening sites advocating tidying the garden, because they know that many people can't tolerate a scruffy garden over winter.

Poverty is also a problem. It is difficult to think about Nature when you are struggling to feed your family or have nowhere to live. Many people are focusing on day to day living and have little time to think about Nature or climate change. The sad thing is that the decline in our environment and climate is only going to create more poverty, but people can't see this and often feel it doesn't or won't affect them.

In your opinion, what is the best way for people to get in tune with Nature?

If you have a garden, start treating it as a Nature reserve and watch what happens. Put cameras out to see who your nightly visitors are, bird feeders, water, untidy hedges, etc. Then go out and look.

Read books, follow wildlife-friendly sites. Become a member of an organisation that supports wildlife like the Wildlife Trusts.

When out, even in a park, look for signs of wildlife and their struggle to survive in a predominantly human environment. If you see an insect you don't know, look it up. Just look.

Also, start young.

I think the first thing we did when we left hospital with our son as a baby, was go for a walk.

When he was little, we spent a lot of time out in Nature with him, going for walks and showing him things. Even as a teenager, although sometimes with a bit of a grudge, he would join us for walks, and he always has had a love and a sensitivity of animals. He grew up with chickens, horses, and dogs, and is very much in tune with Nature. I did actively encourage it. It was very important for me that he was aware of Nature and was a part of Nature because it was so much a part of me. There's no way I would have had children if I didn't have the facilities that I was able to offer him, I just wanted to give him as many different experiences of Nature as possible.

Mostly, I think people need to approach Nature with the view of not, "What can Nature do for me?", but "What can I do for Nature?". This is fundamentally where I think we are wrong at the moment. People want Nature to work for them. We need to work for Nature or there won't be any to connect to.

PART FOUR

THE DISCONNECTION FROM NATURE

"What would our lives be like if our days and nights were as immersed in Nature as they are in technology?"

Richard Louv
American author and journalist

"Life is better when we are in touch with our planet. And when we connect with Nature, we are letting ourselves understand it, and thereby helping to save it".

This quote is from Erik Solheim, United Nations Under Secretary General and UN Environment Executive Director. Erik grew up in Norway and as a child, he developed a deep love for Nature that he still carries with him. His quote has so much meaning, as our disconnection from Nature is at the core of our environmental crisis. More than half the population on our planet live in urban areas and many people have reduced access to "natural" spaces.

Research has shown that moving to greener urban areas was associated with mental health improvements. As Johann Hari described in his book, Lost Connection – Why You're Depressed and How to Find Hope (2018), being cut off from the natural world can cause depression in humans, just like animals in a zoo for instance that have been taken out of their natural habitat. Or, as Richard Louv describes it, people, who are living in areas without trees or other natural features, will experience a social, physical and psychological impact that is noticeably similar to that of animals that have been taken out of natural environment.

What we need, is what Glenn Albrecht, the Australian Nature philosopher calls "eutierria" (eu = good, tierra = earth), a feeling of oneness with the Earth and its life forces.

Humans are often absorbed by their own problems and lose track of the deeper sense of the essence of life; we are very focused on ourselves. When you are in Nature it is not just about you, your ego shrinks, you are feeling tiny in an immense world, you will notice your surroundings more and forget about your worries. It is as if Nature is giving you a new perspective. As I mentioned in Part One, the love of life and all living things is partially in our genes and there is no escape, we are genetically attracted to Nature.

What is causing the disconnection from Nature?

The disconnection from Nature started a long time ago and it has been a gradual process.

As you can read in Dr Jenny Goodman's story in Part Three, modern society started losing its connection with Nature about 200 or 300 years ago, with the industrial revolution. But in actual fact that process has been going on for the last 10,000 years. Because until 10,000 years ago, which is very recent with regard to our biological evolution, we were hunter gatherers and we lived in the forest. At that point, for reasons we still do not understand completely, some hunter gatherers stopped hunting and gathering, and began domesticating plants and animals. They started settling down to turn into agriculturalists or pastoralists, instead of catching wild animals and picking wild plants.

Fast-forward to today and other drivers of disconnection have become clear.

Urbanisation

More than half the people on this planet live in urban areas with limited access to Nature and this number is still going up, with more and more people worldwide moving from rural areas to cities. In 2022 Tokyo had 37,274,000 residents, which is 1,000,000 more than the entire population of Saudi Arabia!

Our modern lifestyle

Nowadays many people live a very sedentary lifestyle, spending a lot of time indoors. From an evolutionary point of view, we are neglecting our needs of being outdoors and being physical. Our ancestors were continuously on the go, hunting, foraging, finding shelter or fending off threats. But many people are more interested in their smart phones and fast food, a life based on convenience, and we have too many distractions. Economic forces are at play in all this too (progress, money etc.). Many people are just too busy to spend time in Nature.

Destruction of Nature

Air and water pollution, deforestation, raiding natural resources, just to name a few, can destroy part of or a whole ecosystem, wiping out the plants and animals that live in those natural habitats. What connection is possible if there is not much left?

Eco-anxiety

The charity Friends of the Earth describes eco-anxiety as *the negative feelings – including stress, fear, anger, and grief – many of us have about climate breakdown, Nature loss and the future of our planet.* It is a fast-growing phenomenon that affects many people, in particular youngsters. According to Save the Children, in 2022, 70% of British children were worried about the world they will inherit. They feel powerless.

Last year the University of East Anglia teamed up with a mental health charity to create a course of six weekly two-hour sessions for students who are suffering from eco-anxiety.

Technology

Our modern society is a technology-intense environment with many forms of indoor and virtual distraction.

In 2022, the average daily media use among internet users in the UK was 5 hours and 47 minutes, using the internet via any device. About 2 hours was spent on social media, 1 hour was spent gaming and on average 2 hours and 24 minutes was spent watching live TV.

We all know the impact of the mobile phone. How often do you see people walking outdoors, looking at their phones (and risking walking into a lamp post)? I wasn't joking about the lamp post by the way, as apparently 17% of all adults in the US have reported bumping into something while texting and walking. Enough said.

As we know, these tech devices often expose us to more sensory information than our brain can process. Wouldn't you prefer to see greenery and listen to the sounds of Nature such as wind, water, or birds?

And then there is the light exposure in the evening. The blue light that is emitted from your computer screen and other devices is disturbing our natural, circadian rhythm by telling our body it is day because of the light exposure and we are disturbing the natural wave of melatonin, that should be increasing at this time of the day and making us feel sleepy.

Technology can't fully replace Nature.

In 2008 Peter Kahn Jr., Professor in the Department of Psychology and Director of the Human Interaction with Nature and Technological Systems (HINTS) Lab and his colleagues researched technological Nature versus real Nature. They installed a camera on top of a building and then showed the actual view of Nature on digital screen "windows". They looked at physical and psychological responses of people looking at the technological Nature window versus looking at Nature through a normal glass window, or no window at all. What they found was that looking at the technological Nature window was less revitalising than looking out of a normal glass window. Although there was no difference between the technological window and no window, other research showed that installing the technological windows in a windowless office had beneficial effects on mental well-being, cognitive function, and the feeling of being connected to Nature.

In 2017 some very interesting research was done on our growing disconnection from Nature by Selin Kesebir PhD, assistant professor of organisational behaviour at London Business School, and Pelin Kesebir PhD, assistant scientist at the Center for Healthy Minds at the University of Wisconsin. They studied works of popular culture in English (books, songs, and movies) from the 20th century and later, and what they found was that from the 1950s onwards Nature featured less and less in popular culture.

The way they researched this is remarkable. They made a list of 186 Nature-related words: general words like cloud, spring, etc., names of flowers, trees and birds, and checked how often these words appeared in books, songs, and movies. The result was that Nature featured a lot less today than before the 1950s. Authors, songwriters, and filmmakers seem to have less connection with Nature nowadays. Is it a coincidence that in the 1950s people first started to watch TV? I don't think so.

Why is the disconnection from Nature so worrying?

As described in Part One Nature & Health, being disconnected from Nature is detrimental to our physical and mental health and well-being. Being disconnected from Nature also means missing out on beauty, happiness, and the feeling of awe, which would increase our sense of connectedness with Nature.

Connectedness to Nature positively affects pro-environmental and responsible behaviour. If we can't see what we have been doing to our planet and are disconnected from Nature, there is little hope. What damage has been done? What consequences did this have for our planet? And what dangers are we facing?

There is need for greater awareness and fortunately it is slowly growing.

As Zylstra et al (2014) say, "CWN [connectedness with Nature] is more than the simple contact or superficial enjoyment of Nature: it is an enduring appreciation, empathy, and mindfulness of the intrinsic value and shared essence of all life…".

Nature-Deficit Disorder

We can't talk about disconnection from Nature without mentioning the term 'Nature-Deficit Disorder'. This term first appeared in Richard Louv's book *Last Child in the Woods – Saving our children from Nature-deficit disorder* (2005) and it refers to the alienation of society from Nature, and what the consequences are: the shrinking of our sensory world, more health issues, negative effects on child development, the suppressing of the creative instinct, an increase in ADHD diagnoses, etc. Children are born naturalists and we should do anything to nurture that, so they can feel connected with Nature throughout their life. Unfortunately, many children have been deprived of time outdoors to explore and connect with Nature.

When you read the stories in Part Three, you will find that virtually all the people I interviewed had great memories of their childhood and the full-on sensory experiences they had in Nature. This has set them all up to have great respect for and a deep connection with Nature.

"Earth and sky, woods and fields, lakes and rivers, the mountain and the sea, are excellent schoolmasters, and teach some of us more than we can ever learn from books."

John Lubbock
English banker, Liberal politician, philanthropist, scientist and polymath

PART FIVE

HOW TO (RE)CONNECT WITH NATURE

*"Nurture your felt love for Nature. Never deny it.
That love is the eons, the purifying intelligence, beauty, and diversity
of Nature sustaining us in its perfection. Our disconnection from this
love and its advice produces our hurt, greed, and destructiveness.
We must reconnect and restore its peaceful voice in
our thoughts, soul, and surroundings"*

Michael J Cohen
Applied Ecopsychologist

Although I have described a bit of the doom and gloom about Nature and people's disconnection from it, there is still hope. The stories you have read in Part Three are good examples. And there is a lot happening in the UK and the rest of the world. People have become more aware of the necessity of the (re)connection with Nature to save our planet and our future. After all, Nature underpins our very existence, we are an intrinsic part of Nature. As Albert Howard put it, "The health of the soil, plant, animal, and man is one and indivisible", and the best way to overcome disconnection is to connect. Nature's recovery depends on us and what we desperately need are changes in human behaviour.

A very recent, large-scale initiative is a good example of hope for the future and changing behaviour. As we know, years of damage have badly affected the UK's wildlife and wild areas. As this Nature catastrophe affects everyone, everyone should have a say about how we should resolve the problems. That's why the World Wide Fund for Nature (WWF), the Royal Society for the Protection of Birds (RSPB) and the National Trust, the UK's leading Nature conservation charities, came up with a plan. In 2022 they created the People's Plan for Nature (PPN) which brought together people from all different backgrounds and asked them about their hopes for Nature and to share known examples of how people can unite to protect and restore Nature. The People's Assembly for Nature was set up with about 100 people, representing a cross-section of the UK population. The PPN is the voice of the UK people.

The People's Assembly for Nature put together 26 calls for action, aimed at national governments, local governments, charities and NGOs, businesses, individuals, and communities. They also produced vision statements for the future of UK's Nature.

One of the calls for action is a national conversation on how and why we should change our diets to support Nature, a subject very close to my heart.

If you are interested in the PPN or would like to get involved, you can add your voice on the PPN website https://peoplesplanforNature.org/

In 2020 the National Trust together with the University of Derby published the *Noticing Nature Report*. A survey was done among 2,096 adults and more than 1,000 children to find out about their connection with Nature, for instance looking at their attitude towards Nature and finding out if they were involved in Nature activities or pro-Nature conservation projects.

49% of the adults and 55% of the children mentioned that they are more worried about Nature and wildlife than they were the previous year. However, when you look at the outcomes of the survey there is still a long way to go…

For example, 90% of the children (versus 57% of the adults) rarely or never watched a sunrise and 77% rarely or never listened to birdsong (versus 62% of the adults). Spending time outdoors doesn't necessarily mean that people will take conservation action. It is what you do while being outdoors that makes the difference. Noticing Nature, like watching a sunrise or listening to birdsong, is more likely to make people take action to help Nature.

The *Noticing Nature Report* is fascinating to read, and I urge you to have a look to see how rare and low participation in Nature activities is and what the National Trust's proposed action plan is. You can find the link to the report in the references list.

There are many ways to (re)connect and forge or rekindle a new relationship with Nature, it is never too late.

What follows is a non-exhaustive list with suggestions; take your pick.

Food

- Ask yourself the question, "Where is my food coming from?"
- Appreciate what it takes to grow food.
- Have a moment of reflection when you are eating.
- Eat and prepare food mindfully.
- Make conscious food choices.
- Grow some of your own food. Even if you don't have a garden, there are still ways to grow your own food. You can grow many different foods such as tomatoes, cucumbers, beans, herbs, etc. in pots, big or small, on patios, window ledges and balconies. Imagine drinking a herbal tea with herbs you grew yourself!

Photo by Kerry J https://kerryjphotography.co.uk/

- Join a community garden or allotment society. Getting in tune with Nature can also happen through other people; when you see someone enjoying Nature, it is contagious. Working together as a group in a garden or on an allotment brings the community together.
- Eat seasonally as much as you can, how Nature intended. Ask yourself, "What is the earth producing during this season?" and try to go for those products.
- Top up your vitamin D level by being outdoors in the sun.
- Go foraging, it is fun and a great way to (re)connect with Nature. This activity is a combination of fresh air, exercise, being close to Nature and ending up with some edibles. It is also a seasonal activity that will show you different wild foods at different times of the year. However, when you are foraging, please be absolutely sure about what you are foraging, as there are so many 'look-alikes' out there that could be poisonous!
- Eat organic food if possible.
- Realise that food becomes part of you after you have eaten. We do not absorb the food; we absorb the nutrients. That is how closely food connects you to Nature.

Use all your senses

- When you're outdoors, put your phone away, open your eyes and pay attention to your surroundings.
- Listen to the sounds of Nature. There is nothing more soothing than birdsong, the sound of crashing waves of the ocean, the babbling of a stream or the rustling of leaves. Research has shown that Nature's sounds reduce anxiety and stress, and they improve your memory and concentration. You can even listen at home to Nature's sounds through relaxation Apps like Calm, that have beautiful soundscapes, but of course you'll be missing out on Nature's other benefits when you're listening indoors.

"The earth has music for those who listen"

William Shakespeare
English playwright

- Go outside and look up into the sky regularly; cloud spotting or stargazing, there is a lot going on overhead during the day and at night. Don't forget the sunrises and sunsets!

- Smell the wildflowers, the roses, the pine trees, the sea air, etc., and enjoy the smells. Many natural fragrances have health benefits, like the relaxing effect of lavender or the calming effect of the pine tree. Using essential oils at home will bring Nature closer.
- Walk barefoot and feel the ground beneath your feet, like the sand or the grass.
  Earthing or grounding connects the body to the Earth's natural field of negatively charged free electrons and this electrically conductive contact has positive effects on the body such as reducing inflammation.
- Watch wildlife in your garden, a park, the woods, wherever you get the chance to see it. Birdwatching, game drives if you are lucky enough to have the chance to go on safari, etc. Watching a wild animal in its own natural habitat is fascinating.
- Exercise outdoors when you can and feel the difference.
- Go Forest Bathing.

Be aware of natural rhythms

- Observe your natural rhythm and your body clock. Adjust your schedule if needed, based on being an early bird or a night owl.
- Avoid or reduce blue light exposure in the evening, turn off your phones, tablets, and computers at least 1-2 hours before bed.
- Become mindful of the darkness, it is an important part of the circadian rhythm.
- Preserve the darkness in your environment; let your garden sit in darkness at night (no flood lights) as light at this time can disrupt and disorientate wildlife, and turn off lights when you leave a room (saves electricity too!).

Activities

- Go hiking or walking, fishing, gardening, or cycling.
- Have a wilderness adventure such as camping.
- Join a litter picking group to clean beaches, etc.

- Participate in Nature-based education: children could join a forest school, a school allotment if available or choose the new Natural History GCSE when the time comes.
- Talk, read and learn about Nature, there is always something new to discover.

To give you an example, I recently learned something interesting about trees.

The forest ecologist Suzanne Simard of the University of British Columbia wrote a book called *Finding the Mother Tree: Discovering the Wisdom of the Forest* (2022). In her book, Simard describes the underground mycorrhizal network, fungi that grow in and around tree roots in a mutually beneficial system, helping trees to communicate and support each other. For example, trees can exchange nutrients or alert each other to environmental threats. I had heard about this before, but actually reading about it made it more real to me.

- Make homes for wildlife in your garden, for insects or hedgehogs for example.
- Take pictures in Nature, there is so much beauty to capture.
- If you are into art, draw or paint scenery, a plant, flower, or animal. Or create Nature mandalas.
- Join a charity or organisation that is involved in protecting Nature, etc. The Woodland Trust, the Soil Association, the World Wide Fund for Nature (WWF, formerly World Wildife Fund), The Wildlife Trusts, Friends of the Earth, the Rainforest Alliance, Green Peace, just to name a few.
- Build a compost box or bin.
- Plant a tree.
- Create a garden, it doesn't matter what size.
- Become a beekeeper.

Children

- Start early, introducing children to Nature and lead by example.

"Children are born with a sense of wonder and an affinity for Nature. Properly cultivated, these values can mature into ecological literacy, and eventually into sustainable patterns of living."

Zenobia Barlow
Executive director and cofounder of the Center for Ecoliteracy, an American nonprofit organisation that supports and progresses education for sustainable living.

- Encourage young people to explore the world by learning about living organisms and environments, environmental and sustainability issues to gain a deeper knowledge of the natural world in which we all live.
- Allow children to love Nature before we ask them to save it.

General recommendations

- Start with something basic and simple like nurturing a pot plant at home.
- Build a habit, something you schedule, if it is something you don't already do.

For instance, schedule a lunch time walk in your diary, and go out no matter what the weather is like. Allow Nature space in your life.

- Be aware of what is around you when you're outdoors and notice Nature.
- Accept Nature with all its imperfection.
- Try to be mindful and take time to be aware of your feelings and your surroundings.

- Find something you love doing outdoors. Finding something you enjoy is the only way to create a life-long habit.
- Approach Nature not with the view of what Nature can do for YOU, but what you can do for NATURE.
- Recognise the need to slow down and take time to be part of Nature, by just being.
- Train your brain: experiences can change the structural organisation of the brain and change the way you feel. Thinking of positive experiences in nature can have a positive impact.
- Reduce your exposure to pollutants and toxicants. Eliminate plastic from your life as much as possible. Chose eco-friendly cleaning products, detergents, and personal care items. By reducing your exposure, you are not just protecting yourself, but you are also doing your bit for the environment and protecting Nature.

Of course, spending 20 minutes in Nature will not save the environment or the planet, but it is a step in the right direction, as even a short period of time outdoors in Nature has advantages for health and well-being and you might acquire a feeling of connection with Nature. It is this feeling of connection that is profoundly associated with environmentally responsible behaviour and concern for Nature.

There is a beautiful quote by the Polish-American Rabbi Abraham Joshua Heschel that says:

> *"Our goal should be to live life in radical amazement, to look at the world in a way that takes nothing for granted. Everything is phenomenal; everything is incredible; never treat life casually. To be spiritual is to be amazed."*

And that is exactly what we should be doing, looking at Nature in amazement, not taking it for granted and not treating it casually, but looking after it.

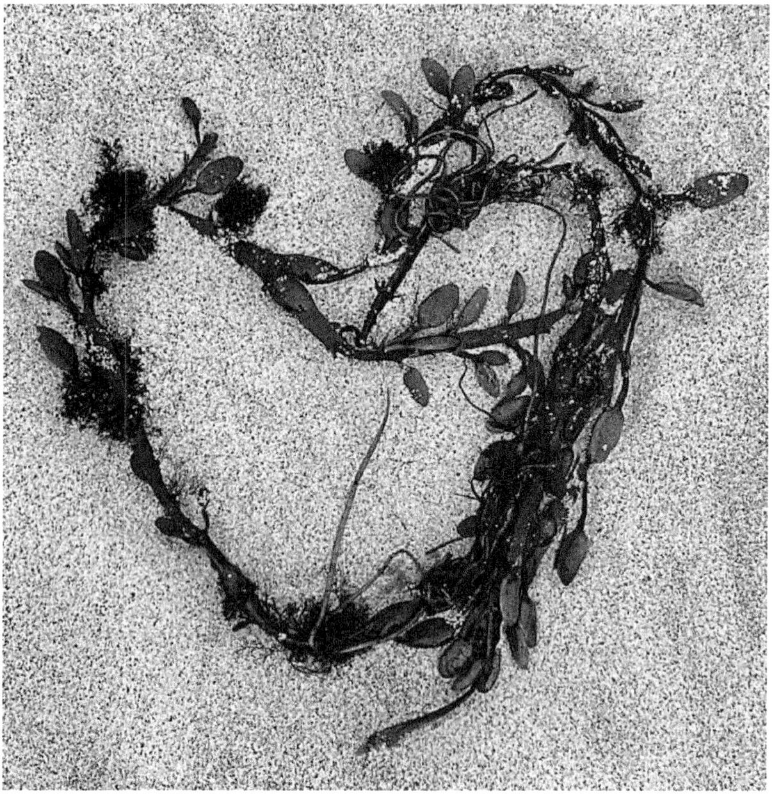

EPILOGUE

I always wanted to write a book and always had a burning desire to put my thoughts on paper. So, I kept diaries from childhood till my late twenties, wrote newsletters whilst living abroad to keep family and friends updated and I actually enjoyed writing assignments while I was studying – *my daughter would have frowned on this as at the time I wrote this she was battling with a huge assignment for her degree course.* Later in life, after having retrained as a nutritional therapist, I started to write blogs and articles about nutrition, some of which were published. So, the logical continuation would have been a book on nutrition. Funnily enough I never aspired to write such a book. Then one night, while lying awake, I suddenly had this brain wave…

When you write a book, it must be on something you're passionate about. Yes, I am passionate about nutrition, but even more so about Nature. What if I could link the two together? I was bouncing with enthusiasm the next morning, but the enthusiasm quickly faded when I started asking myself if I had enough to say about the subject to fill a book.

That day we had a 7-hour ferry crossing to the Netherlands ahead of us, which is pretty boring, so instead of reading a book, I got a piece of paper and started to write down ideas. Before I knew it, I had a list of people I knew, who have a strong connection with Nature and with whom I definitely wanted to engage in conversation to acquire some more input on the subject. I ended up with a list of about 20 people and decided that the best way forward would be to interview them. I compiled a list of questions, emailed everyone, and then sat back and waited for their reactions, not expecting too much because everyone is so busy nowadays. To my great surprise, absolutely everyone I asked reacted positively and enthusiastically, and before I knew it, I had a series of interviews lined up.

These interviews were so inspiring, and it was utterly wonderful to talk about my favourite topic with like-minded people.

While in the process of writing, I met more people who were happy to be involved, sometimes through the most weird and wonderful ways. Like when one of the contributors forgot about the interview and didn't show up (the interview did happen a few days later). When I mentioned this to a friend that same day, I guess she felt a bit sorry for me and she promptly introduced me to a friend of hers, who she thought would be a great asset to the book, given her amazing story. Two days later we were talking, and it was, as promised, a wonderful contribution. Plus, I made a friend for life! (thank you, Sam). Or the moment I told one of my husband's work colleagues in South Africa about the book, and she connected me with the most remarkable couple, who I would never have found myself, given they are living in the middle of nowhere at the Western Cape of South Africa (thank you, Hannelie!).

Along the way I learned a lot, especially about farming (thanks Guy and Fred!), but I also made new friends and shared some deep emotions with some of the contributors.

More than anything, it showed me that we all have our stories, and that life is what we make of it.

I'm deeply grateful to all the people who so generously gave their time and shared their story with me. You are an inspiration and I do hope that the readers of this book will follow your advice and become as passionate about Nature as you are.

As the writing of this book is coming to a close, I'm having mixed feelings. On the one hand I'm feeling elated that I managed to finish the manuscript. On the other hand, I will miss the interviews, the research, and the actual writing, so I guess another book will have to follow eventually.

"Love what you do and do what you love.
Passion is the key that opens the door to joy and abundance."

David Cuschieri
American author

ACKNOWLEDGEMENTS

I always thought that writing a book is a lonely affair. How wrong I was…

This exciting journey has been all about human connection. So, I would like to express my gratitude to all the wonderful human beings who helped me creating this book to get the message out into the world:

- My endlessly patient husband David and daughter Alyssa for their emotional and practical support. I bet you can't wait to see what Mum is up to next!
- All the friends who believed in me and supported me where they could, especially Solveig who prepared me for the world of publishing (you were 100% right).
- My incredible editor Marion Cooper, who not only went through the manuscript with a fine-tooth comb, but also cheered me on with her infectious enthusiasm.
- Balboa Press UK for answering my numerous questions and getting this book out in the world.
- All the inspiring contributors who very kindly gave me their time and their stories. Without you this book would not exist!
Thank you Abby, Andrew, Charlie, Daniel, Daria & Heine, Ed, Élise, Emily, Fred, Guy, Jenny, Jim, Joe, Lou, Mariel & Gerbrand, Marion, Mel, Olivier, Orli, Phoebe, Sophie, Susan, Thinley, Tone, Victoria and 'Zarah'.
- My Nutritional Therapy clients who motivated me to write this book to help them on their journey to better health and well-being.
- All the researchers and authors who helped me increase my knowledge and enthused me even more about the subject.

REFERENCES

IT ALL STARTED WITH THE COSMOS

Allen, R. (2021). Grounded. page 17. London, Mortimer Books

INTRODUCTION

Emerson (1909) Nature. New York: Duffield.

Louv, R. (2011). The Nature principle: human restoration and the end of Nature-deficit disorder. Page 6. Chapel Hill, N.C.: Algonquin Books of Chapel Hill

Richardson, M. et al (2020). The green care code: How Nature connectedness and simple activities help explain pro-Nature conservation behaviours. People and Nature. 2020; 2: 821– 839. https://doi.org/10.1002/pan3.10117

PART ONE – NATURE AND HEALTH

Viriditas: the greening power of the Divine (or Divine Healing Power of Green) https://www.healthyhildegard.com/ Accessed online December 2022

NATURAL RHYTHMS

Adan, A. (1994), Chronotype and personality factors in the daily consumption of alcohol and psychostimulants. *Addiction*, 89: 455-462. https://doi.org/10.1111/j.1360-0443.1994.tb00926.x Abstract

Anderson, J. et al (1994). Sleep in fall/winter seasonal affective disorder: effects of light and changing seasons. *Journal of Psychosomatic Research*, 38(4), 323–337. https://doi.org/10.1016/0022-3999(94)90037-x

Ciarleglio, C. M., Resuehr, H. E., & McMahon, D. G. (2011). Interactions of the serotonin and circadian systems: Nature and nurture in rhythms and blues. *Neuroscience*, 197, 8–16. https://doi.org/10.1016/j.neuroscience.2011.09.036
Abstract

Circadian Rhythms https://nigms.nih.gov/education/fact-sheets/Pages/circadian-rhythms.aspx
Accessed online January 2023

Copinschi, G. et al (1999). Les rythmes biologiques. Rythmes circadiens, ultradiens et saisonniers. [Biological rhythms. Circadian, ultradian and seasonal rhythms]. *Presse Medicale* (Paris, France : 1983), 28(17), 933–935. https://pubmed.ncbi.nlm.nih.gov/10360194/ Abstract

Eklöf, J. (2022). The Darkness Manifesto - How Light Pollution Threatens the Ancient Rhythms of Life. P161. London, The Bodley Head

Gale C. & Martyn C. (1998). Larks and owls and health, wealth, and wisdom. *British Medical Journal* 1998; 317 :1675
https://www.bmj.com/content/317/7174/1675

Geddes, L. (2019). Why we should be watching the sun, not the clock. https://amp.theguardian.com/news/2019/jan/11/watching-the-sun-not-the-clock-sleep-body-clocks-daylight-saving-time
Accessed online January 2023

Gnocchi, D., & Bruscalupi, G. (2017). Circadian Rhythms and Hormonal Homeostasis: Pathophysiological Implications. *Biology*, 6(1), 10. https://doi.org/10.3390/biology6010010

Iglesia, de la, H. O., & Johnson, C. H. (2013). Biological clocks: riding the tides. *Current Biology* 23(20), R921–R923. https://doi.org/10.1016/j.cub.2013.09.006

Jones, S. et al (2019). Genome-wide association analyses of chronotype in 697,828 individuals provides insights into circadian rhythms. *Nature Communications* 10, 343 (2019). https://doi.org/10.1038/s41467-018-08259-7

National Tidal and Sea Level Facility. All about tides. https://ntslf.org/about-tides/tides Accessed online January 2023

Oravec, M. & Greenham, K. (2022). The adaptive Nature of the plant circadian clock in natural environments, *Plant Physiology*, Volume 190, Issue 2, October 2022, 968–980. https://doi.org/10.1093/plphys/kiac337

Peschel, N. & Helfrich-Förster, C. (2011). Setting the clock – by Nature: Circadian rhythm in the fruitfly *Drosophila melanogaster*. *FEBS Letters*, 2011, 1435-1442, https://doi.org/10.1016/j.febslet.2011.02.028

Seasonal Affective Disorder https://www.nimh.nih.gov/health/publications/seasonal-affective-disorder Accessed online January 2023

Stothard, E. et al (2017). Circadian Entrainment to the Natural Light-Dark Cycle across Seasons and the Weekend. *Current Biology* : CB, 27(4), 508–513. https://doi.org/10.1016/j.cub.2016.12.041

OUR CONNECTION WITH NATURE

Asprey, D. This Fractal Video Will Lower Your Stress By 60% In a Matter Of Seconds https://daveasprey.com/fractal-lower-stress/ Accessed online January 2023

Lohr, V. I. (2007). Benefits of Nature: what we are learning about why people respond to Nature. *Journal of Physiological Anthropology*, 26(2), 83–85. https://doi.org/10.2114/jpa2.26.83

Lohr, V. I. & Pearson-Mims C. H. (2016). Responses to Scenes with Spreading, Rounded, and Conical Tree Forms. *Environment and Behaviour* https://doi.org/10.1177/00139165062873

Metzner, R. (1995). The Psychopathology of the Human-Nature Relationship. *Essay*
https://www.webpages.uidaho.edu/rrt_psyc504/readings/psychopathology%20of%20human-Nature.pdf
Accessed online January 2023

Rogers, K. (2019). "biophilia hypothesis". *Encyclopedia Britannica* https://www.britannica.com/science/biophilia-hypothesis
Accessed online January 2023

Seymour, V. (2016). The Human–Nature Relationship and Its Impact on Health: A Critical Review. *Front. Public Health* https://doi.org/10.3389/fpubh.2016.00260

Simion, M. (2016). Fractal images – a new way to reduce stress and to improve educational workspaces. *Global Journal of Psychology Research*. 6(1), 20-30.
https://un-pub.eu/ojs/index.php/gjpr/article/view/477

Taylor, R. Department of Physics, University of Oregon
https://uonews.uoregon.edu/richard-taylor-department-physics

Wulf, A. (2015). The Invention of Nature: Alexander Von Humboldt's New World. New York, Alfred A. Knopf

Hansen, M., Jones & Tocchini, K. (2017). Shinrin-Yoku (Forest Bathing) and Nature Therapy: A State-of-the-Art Review. *International Journal of Environmental Research and Public Health* 2017, 14, 851. https://doi.org/10.3390/ijerph14080851

Kotera, Y., Richardson, M. & Sheffield, D. (2022). Effects of Shinrin-Yoku (Forest Bathing) and Nature Therapy on Mental Health: a Systematic Review and Meta-analysis. *International Journal of Mental Health and Addiction* 20, 337–361. https://doi.org/10.1007/s11469-020-00363-4

Li Q. (2010). Effect of forest bathing trips on human immune function. *Environmental Health and Preventive Medicine*, 15(1), 9–17. https://doi.org/10.1007/s12199-008-0068-3

McEwan, K. et al (2021). A Pragmatic Controlled Trial of Forest Bathing Compared with Compassionate Mind Training in the UK: Impacts on Self-Reported Wellbeing and Heart Rate Variability. *Sustainability* 13(3), 1380; https://doi.org/10.3390/su13031380

Oh, K. H. et al (2020). Six-Step Model of Nature-Based Therapy Process. *International Journal of Environmental Research and Public Health*, 17(3), 685. https://doi.org/10.3390/ijerph17030685

Park, S. et al (2021). Evidence-Based Status of Forest Healing Program in South Korea. *International Journal of Environmental Research and Public Health*, 18(19), 10368. https://doi.org/10.3390/ijerph181910368

Song, C., Ikei, H., & Miyazaki, Y. (2016). Physiological Effects of Nature Therapy: A Review of the Research in Japan. *International Journal of Environmental Research and Public Health*, 13(8), 781. https://doi.org/10.3390/ijerph13080781

MENTAL HEALTH

Oh, K. H. et al (2020). Six-Step Model of Nature-Based Therapy Process. *International Journal of Environmental Research and Public Health, 17*(3), 685. https://doi.org/10.3390/ijerph17030685

Lederbogen, F. et al (2011). City living and urban upbringing affect neural social stress processing in humans. *Nature* 474, 498–501 (2011). https://doi.org/10.1038/Nature10190 Abstract

STRESS

Overview of Urban Development
https://www.worldbank.org/en/topic/urbandevelopment/overview

Dockrill, P. (2015). Access to Nature May Be Vital For Mental Health, Study Finds
https://www.sciencealert.com/access-to-Nature-may-be-vital-for-mental-health-study-finds

Lederbogen, F. et al (2011). City living and urban upbringing affect neural social stress processing in humans. *Nature* 474, 498–501 (2011). https://doi.org/10.1038/Nature10190 Abstract

Berman, M. G. et al (2012). Interacting with Nature Improves Cognition and Affect for Individuals with Depression. *Journal of Affective Disorders*, 140(3), 300–305. https://doi.org/10.1016/j.jad.2012.03.012

Madhuleena Roy Chowdhury, M. (2019). The Positive Effects Of Nature On Your Mental Wellbeing https://positivepsychology.com/positive-effects-of-Nature/

Ulrich, R.S. (1984), View Through a Window May Influence Recovery from Surgery.

Science, 420-421. https://doi.org/10.1126/science.6143402 Abstract

Maas J. et al (2006). Green space, urbanity, and health: how strong is the relation? *Journal of Epidemiology and Community Health,* 60, 587–592. https://pubmed.ncbi.nlm.nih.gov/16790830/

Sudimac, S., Sale, V. & Kühn, S. (2022). How Nature nurtures: Amygdala activity decreases as the result of a one-hour walk in Nature. *Molecular Psychiatry,* 27, 4446–4452.
https://doi.org/10.1038/s41380-022-01720-6

Gruebner, O. et al (2017). Cities and Mental Health. *Deutsches Arzteblatt International.* 2017 Feb;114(8):121-127. https://europepmc.org/article/PMC/5374256

Clatworthy, J., Hinds, J., & Camic, P. M. (2013). Gardening as a mental health intervention: A review. *Mental Health Review Journal.* https://doi.org/10.1108/MHRJ-02-2013-0007 Abstract

Harris, H. (2017). The social dimensions of therapeutic horticulture. *Health & Social Care in the Community,* 25(4), 1328-1336. https://doi.org/10.1111/hsc.12433
Abstract

The Green Hub Project for Teens: https://greenhub.org.uk/

PART TWO - NATURE AND NUTRITION

Milliron, B. J. et al (2022). Nature Relatedness Is Positively Associated With Dietary Diversity and Fruit and Vegetable Intake in an Urban Population. *American Journal of Health Promotion* 36(6), 1019–1024. https://doi.org/10.1177/08901171221086941

FOOD WASTE

Aleksandrowicz, L. et al (2016. The Impacts of Dietary Change on Greenhouse Gas Emissions, Land Use, Water Use, and Health: A

Systematic Review. *PLOS ONE* 11(11): e0165797. https://doi.org/10.1371/journal.pone.0165797

The British Nutrition Foundation *What is a healthy, sustainable diet?* https://www.nutrition.org.uk/healthy-sustainable-diets/ Accessed online January 2023

World Economic Forum. 2021. *The world's food waste problem is bigger than we thought - here's what we can do about it.* https://www.weforum.org/agenda/2021/03/global-food-waste-solutions Accessed online January 2023

FAO, IFAD, UNICEF, WFP and WHO. 2020. In Brief to The State of Food Security and Nutrition in the World 2021. Transforming food systems for food security, improved nutrition and affordable healthy diets for all. Rome, FAO https://doi.org/10.4060/cb5409en

World Health Organization (2022). *UN Report: Global hunger numbers rose to as many as 828 million in 2021.* https://www.who.int/news/item/06-07-2022-un-report--global-hunger-numbers-rose-to-as-many-as-828-million-in-2021 Accessed online December 2022

The EAT- Lancet Commission on Food, Planet, Health (2019). *Can we feed a future population of 10 billion people a healthy diet within planetary boundaries?* https://eatforum.org/content/uploads/2019/07/EAT-Lancet_Commission_Summary_Report.pdf Accessed online December 2022

Marshman, J., & Scott, S. (2019). Gleaning in the 21st Century: Urban food recovery and community food security in Ontario, Canada. Canadian Food Studies / La Revue Canadienne Des études Sur l'Alimentation, 6(1), 100–119. https://doi.org/10.15353/cfs-rcea.v6i1.264

GLEANING

https://gleaning.feedbackglobal.org/go-gleaning/

https://www.ukharvest.org.uk/

https://www.foodcycle.org.uk

Marshman, J., & Scott, S. (2019). Gleaning in the 21st Century: Urban food recovery and community food security in Ontario, Canada. Canadian Food Studies / La Revue Canadienne Des études Sur l'Alimentation, 6(1), 100–119. https://doi.org/10.15353/cfs-rcea.v6i1.264

Stevenson, R. (2022). Why the ancient art of gleaning is making a comeback across England. The Guardian. https://www.theguardian.com/environment/2022/feb/19/harvest-for-all-why-ancient-art-of-gleaning-is-making-a-comeback-food-banks-food-waste

GROWING YOUR OWN FOOD

Garcia, M. et al (2018). The impact of urban gardens on adequate and healthy food: A systematic review. *Public Health Nutrition*, 21(2), 416-425. https://doi.org/10.1017/S1368980017002944

Kim, S. O., & Park, S. A. (2020). Garden-Based Integrated Intervention for Improving Children's Eating Behavior for Vegetables. *International Journal of Environmental Research and Public Health*, 17(4), 1257. https://doi.org/10.3390/ijerph17041257

CHRONONUTRITION

Arola-Arnal A. et al (2019). Chrononutrition and Polyphenols: Roles and Diseases. *Nutrients* 11(11):2602. https://doi.org/10.3390/nu11112602

Flanagan, A. et al (2021). Chrono-nutrition: From molecular and neuronal mechanisms to human epidemiology and timed feeding patterns. *Journal of Neurochemistry*, 157: 53– 72. https://doi.org/10.1111/jnc.15246

Institute for Functional Medicine Chronobiology: The Dynamic Field of Rhythm and Clock Genes https://www.ifm.org/news-insights/chronobiology-dynamic-field-rhythm-clock-genes/ Accessed March 2023

Newman, T. & Jospe, M. (2022), Chrononutrition: Does it matter when you eat? https://joinzoe.com/learn/what-is-chrononutrition.amp

Pot, G.K. (2021). Chrono-nutrition – an emerging, modifiable risk factor for chronic disease? *Nutrition Bulletin*, 46: 114-119. https://doi.org/10.1111/nbu.12498

Stephan F. K. (2002). The "other" circadian system: food as a Zeitgeber. *Journal of Biological Rhythms*, 17(4), 284–292. https://doi.org/10.1177/074873040201700402

Wilson, J. E. et al (2020), An eating pattern characterised by skipped or delayed breakfast is associated with mood disorders among an Australian adult cohort. *Psychological Medicine*, 50 (16). pp. 2711-2721. https://doi.org/10.1017/S0033291719002800

HEALTHY SOIL, HEALTHY FOOD

https://civileats.com/2022/12/01/soil-health-is-human-health/
Accessed online March 2023

Davis, D. et al (2004). Changes in USDA food composition data for 43 garden crops, 1950 to 1999. *Journal of the American College of Nutrition*, 23(6), 669–682. https://doi.org/10.1080/07315724.2004.10719409

Montgomery, D. & Biklé, A. (2022). *What Your Food Ate: How to Restore Our Land and Reclaim Our Health.* New York, W. W. Norton & Company

Soil Association (2022). The 'magic' of soil: what is the importance of soil in agriculture, and what can farmers do to protect it?, https://www.soilassociation.org/blogs/2022/january/20/the-magic-of-soil-what-is-the-importance-of-soil-in-agriculture-and-what-can-farmers-do-to-protect-it/

Soil depletion and what it means to you. https://naturallysavvy.com/restore/soil-depletion-and-what-it-means-to-you/
Accessed online January 2023

https://www.sustainweb.org/
Accessed online March 2023

SEASONAL EATING

Beattie, A. (1999). *Seasonal Living - A Guide to living in harmony with Nature and the seasons.* London Parkgate Books

Khatsenkova, S. for Euronews.green (2023). *Fact check: Is Brexit to blame for Britain's fruit and vegetable shortages?* https://www.euronews.com/green/2023/02/24/fact-check-is-brexit-to-blame-for-britains-fruit-and-vegetable-shortages

Singh-Watson, G. (2023). *How to bridge the UK's Hungry Gap.* https://wickedleeks.riverford.co.uk/opinion/how-to-bridge-the-uks-hungry-gap/ Accessed online February 2023

VITAMIN 'SUNSHINE'

Aspray, T.J. et al (2014), 'National Osteoporosis Society Vitamin D guideline summary', *Age Ageing*, 2014 Sep;43(5):592-5 https://www.ncbi.nlm.nih.gov/pubmed/25074538

Craig, A. & Elmets, M.D. reviewing Terushkin, V. et al (2010), How much sunlight is equivalent to vitamin D supplementation?, *Journal of the American Academy of Dermatology*, 2010 June. http://www.jwatch.org/jd201006040000002/2010/06/04/how-much-sunlight-equivalent-vitamin-d

Gómez, A. et al (2003), Review of the concept of vitamin D "sufficiency and insufficiency". *Nefrologia* 2003;23 Suppl. 2:73-7. https://www.ncbi.nlm.nih.gov/pubmed/12778859

BREAST MILK

Lahdenperä, M. et al. (2023), Residential green environments are associated with human milk oligosaccharide diversity and composition. *Science Reports* 13, 216. https://doi.org/10.1038/s41598-022-27317-1

FORAGING

Renton, M. & Biggane, E. (2022). *Foraging Pocket Guide.* UK Otherwise Publishing Ltd.

Iverson, C. (2019). *The Hedgerow Apothecary.* London, Summersdale Publishers Ltd.

King, A. & Marshall, H. (2022). Optimal foraging. *Current Biology* : CB, 32(12), R680–R683. https://doi.org/10.1016/j.cub.2022.04.072

FOOD MILES

Allen, P. *The facts about food miles.* https://www.bbcgoodfood.com/howto/guide/facts-about-food-miles
Accessed online March 2023

Foodmiles.com. *Food Miles Calculator.*
https://www.foodmiles.com/

Howell, B. (2023). *What Are 'Food Miles' And How Can You Reduce Them?*
https://www.theecoexperts.co.uk/home-hub/food-miles
Accessed online March 2023

Li, M. et al. Global food-miles account for nearly 20% of total food-systems emissions. *Nat Food* **3**, 445–453 (2022). https://doi.org/10.1038/s43016-022-00531-w Abstract

Milner J. et al (2015). Health effects of adopting low greenhouse gas emission diets in the UK. *British Medical Journal Open* 2015 5:e007364. https://bmjopen.bmj.co m/content/5/4/e007364.long

Spector, T. (2020). *Spoonfed - Why Almost Everything We've Been Told About Food is Wrong.* 207-215, London, Jonathan Cape

PollutionIssues (2008). *Food Miles: The Environmental Impact of Food.* https://pollutionissues.co.uk/food-miles-environmental-impact-food/
Accessed online March 2023

Searchinger, T. D., Wirsenius, S., Beringer, T., & Dumas, P. (2018). Assessing the efficiency of changes in land use for mitigating climate change. *Nature*, 564 (7735), 249–253. https://doi.org/10.1038/s41586-018-0757-z Abstract

Stylianou, N. et al for BBC Science & Environment (2019). *Climate change food calculator: What's your diet's carbon footprint?* https://www.bbc.co.uk/news/science-environment-46459714
Accessed online March 2023

The Ethical Choice. *Food Miles.*
https://www.eta.co.uk/environmental-info/food-miles/
Accessed online March 2023

PART FOUR - THE DISCONNECTION WITH NATURE

Alcock, I. et al (2014). Longitudinal effects on mental health of moving to greener and less green urban areas. *Environmental Science & Technology*, 48(2), 1247–1255. https://doi.org/10.1021/es403688w

Atchley, R., Strayer, D. & Atchley, P. (2012). Creativity in the wild: improving creative reasoning through immersion in natural settings. *PLOS ONE*, 7(12), e51474. https://doi.org/10.1371/journal.pone.0051474

Frumkin, H. et al (2017). Nature Contact and Human Health: A Research Agenda. *Environmental Health Perspectives*, 125(7), 075001. https://doi.org/10.1289/EHP1663

Hari, J. (2018). Lost connections: uncovering the real causes of depression-- and the unexpected solutions. p150-160. New York, Bloomsbury.

Kahn Jr, P. (2020). Losing touch with Nature. *IAI News* Issue 92. https://iai.tv/articles/losing-touch-with-Nature-auid-1683

Kesebir, S. & Kesebir, P. (2017). A Growing Disconnection From Nature Is Evident in Cultural Products. *Perspectives on Psychological Science 12 (2)*. https://doi.org/10.1177/1745691616662473
Accessed online April 2023

Liu, J. et al (2023). Awe of Nature and well-being: Roles of Nature connectedness and powerlessness. *Personality and Individual Differences* 111946. https://doi.org/10.1016/j.paid.2022.111946

Louv, R. (2011). The Nature principle: human restoration and the end of Nature-deficit disorder. Page 63. Chapel Hill, N.C.: Algonquin Books of Chapel Hill

Louv, R. (2005). *Last Child in the Woods - Saving Our Children from Nature-Deficit Disorder.* New York: Algonquin Books of Chapel Hill.

Madden M. & Rainie L. (2010) Adults and cell phone distractions. Washington, DC: *Pew Internet & American Life Project*; https://www.pewresearch.org/internet/2010/06/18/adults-and-cell-phone-distractions/
Accessed online April 2023

McDade, T. W. et al (2009). Early origins of inflammation: microbial exposures in infancy predict lower levels of C-reactive protein in adulthood. *Proceedings of the Royal Society B*, 2771129–1137 http://doi.org/10.1098/rspb.2009.1795

Pihkala, P. (2020). Eco-Anxiety and Environmental Education. *Sustainability* 12 (23). 10149. https://doi.org/10.3390/su122310149

Simard, S. (2022). *Finding the Mother Tree: Discovering the Wisdom of the Forest.* USA, Alfred A. Knopf.

Schiffman, R. (2021). *Mother Trees' Are Intelligent: They Learn and Remember And ecologist Suzanne Simard says they need our help to survive* https://www.scientificamerican.com/article/mother-trees-are-intelligent-they-learn-and-remember/ Accessed online April 2023

Schmidt, B. Leaving Paradise? How we have lost connection to Nature. https://www.positran.eu/leaving-paradise-lost-connection-Nature/ Accessed online March 2023

Zylstra, M. et al (2014). Connectedness as a core conservation concern: An interdisciplinary review of theory and a call for practice. *Springer Science Reviews*, 2(1), 119-143. http://dx.doi.org/10.1007/s40362-014-0021-3

PART FIVE – HOW TO (RE)CONNECT WITH NATURE

Eftaxia, G. (2021). *The Powerful effect of the sound of Nature on human health.* https://www.radioart.com/blog/the-powerful-effect-of-the-sound-of-Nature-on-human-health Accessed online April 2023

Eklöf, J. (2022). The Darkness Manifesto - How Light Pollution Threatens the Ancient Rhythms of Life. London, The Bodley Head

Mandolesi, L. et al (2017). Environmental Factors Promoting Neural Plasticity: Insights from Animal and Human Studies. *Neural plasticity*, 2017, 7219461. https://doi.org/10.1155/2017/7219461

Oschman, J. et al (2015). The effects of grounding (earthing) on inflammation, the immune response, wound healing, and prevention and treatment of chronic inflammatory and autoimmune diseases. *Journal of Inflammation Research*, 8, 83–96. https://doi.org/10.2147/JIR.S69656

Richardson, M. et al (2020) The green care code: How Nature connectedness and simple activities help explain pro-Nature conservation behaviours. *People and Nature,* 2: 821– 839. https://doi.org/10.1002/pan3.10117

The National Trust & University of Derby (2020). *Noticing Nature Report.* https://nt.global.ssl.fastly.net/binaries/content/assets/website/national/pdf/noticingNaturereport_final.pdf Accessed online April 2023

The People's Plan for Nature https://peoplesplanforNature.org/ Accessed online April 2023

ABOUT THE AUTHOR

Monique Parker is a naturopathic nutritional therapist with a private practice, nature-lover, gardener/allotmenteer and beekeeper's wife. She is passionate about nature in all its forms, especially the effects it has on our life, health, and well-being.

Monique has a strong interest in food, not just the growing, cooking and eating of it, but also the issues of our broken food system, and of course the link between food and health.

Originally from the Netherlands, and having lived in Hong Kong, Vietnam, and Saudi Arabia, Monique has lived in the UK since 1999 with her British husband and daughter.

Photo by Kerry J
https://kerryjphotography.co.uk/

Before studying nutrition at the College of Naturopathic Medicine in London, Monique worked in education and Human Resource Management.

Alongside working as a practitioner, Monique writes articles for the media and blogs for her website (www.nutritionforyou.co.uk). Apart from giving talks on health topics such as menopause, immune support, etc. she also runs workshops, as a volunteer, for a charity that provides a therapeutic garden for teenagers with mental health problems.

Printed in Great Britain
by Amazon